Heart *of a* Shepherd

Heart *of a* Shepherd

Meditations for New Pastors

ANGIE BEST-BOSS

Judson Press
Valley Forge

Heart of a Shepherd: Meditations for New Pastors

All names of persons appearing in this book have been changed.

Library of Congress Cataloging-in-Publication Data

Best-Boss, Angie.
Heart of a shepherd : meditations for new pastors / Angie Best-Boss.
p. cm.
Includes index.
ISBN 0-8170-1344-X (pbk. : alk. paper)
1. Clergy Prayer-books and devotions—English. 2. Clergy—Office Meditations. I. Title.
BV4011.6.B435 2000
242'.692—dc21 99-40029

Printed in the U.S.A.

06 05 04 03 02 01 00

10 9 8 7 6 5 4 3 2 1

To the glory of God
and
to my parents,
Sarah and Sam Houston
and
James and Barbara Best

ACKNOWLEDGMENTS

With special thanks to
DuWain and Kaylyn,
for giving me the inspiration
and freedom to write,
and
to Tammy Campbell,
for her friendship, unwavering support,
and encouragement.

CONTENTS

INTRODUCTION

My first few years of full-time ministry were some of the most challenging years of my life. In some ways, this period in life was discouraging and lonely. At other times, it was exciting and fulfilling and everything I had hoped ministry would be. Those early years stretched me in ways I had never before experienced. While I learned much during that time, I wouldn't want to repeat that phase! On the other hand, I don't want to forget the lessons God taught me then, either.

For example, I have had to learn how to gauge success. What did it mean to be a "good pastor"? More importantly, was I one? How should I deal with my own failures? How could I learn to confront my professional weaknesses and personal foibles? For what purpose and to what end had I packed my family into a moving van to move one thousand miles from home to shepherd a struggling flock? Was I making a difference? I desperately wanted to!

I have found that the closer I draw to God, the easier those struggles become. And in the meantime, God has surprised me often. I was surprised by just how much I have grown to love and care for these people to whom God sent me. I was surprised by the people themselves—by their decisions, their inaction, their peculiarities, their prayers, and their love for our family.

I pray that you might learn as well the lessons God longs to teach you—that those lessons would not fall by the wayside, that you would shepherd faithfully. And I pray that you may enjoy the journey as much as I have. May the grace of our Lord Jesus Christ be with you all (1 Thessalonians 5:28, *paraphrase*).

Carrying the cross

Those who love their life lose it, and those who hate their life in this world will keep it for eternal life. Who ever serves me must follow me, and where I am, there will my servant be also. Whoever serves me, the Father will honor.

—JOHN 12:25–27

I GOT IN THE CAR AND SLAMMED THE DOOR. I NEEDED TO GET OUT OF the office for a while, so I decided to make a pastoral call to someone who lived half an hour away. The phone call this morning had surprised me. It had been one member describing a conversation she had had with another—disgruntled—member. The caller let me know of this other member's effect on the state of the church. The caller had defended me, but she wanted me to be aware of the situation.

My mind flashed back to the dozens of times I had supported that unhappy member, and I was simply furious. Surely, I thought, all those hours of ministry at least warranted a call to me sharing her concerns. This was the first major criticism I had received in my new pastorate, and I was devastated. I felt as though I had been hit in the stomach. Shaking my head in disbelief, I turned on the radio for distraction. I was pleased to hear that a favorite radio preacher was on.

"What do you expect your cross to look like?" he asked. "When Jesus says 'Pick up your cross and follow me,' do you ignore him because you can't imagine literally carrying a cross like he did? Maybe you need to think about it more closely and examine where in your life Jesus is wanting you to pick up the cross to follow him more closely."

I clicked off the radio, not wanting to listen to talk about suffering. But as the preacher's words remained embedded in my consciousness, I couldn't help but consider what my cross, my burden for Christ looked like. Did living in a parsonage with orange shag carpet count? How about struggling to live on a pastor's salary?

The answer, however, was clear. For pastors, the cross we carry is the burden of our people—their concerns, their faith struggles, their marriages and jobs, their health, and their salvation. Part of what makes our task a burden is that sometimes our folks are not appreciative of our care and can be hurtful. Sometimes, they are a source of great joy and blessings, and other times they are a responsibility. Nevertheless, they are the flock that God has given to us.

As you faithfully serve your flock, be intentional about rejoicing over those whom God has given to you, entrusting them to your care. ❧

2

Advice well taken

Therefore, since we are surrounded by so great
a cloud of witnesses, let us also lay aside every
weight and the sin that clings so closely, and let us run
with perseverance the race that is set before us.

—HEBREWS 12:1

"NOW, PASTOR, I DON'T WANT YOU TAKE THIS THE WRONG WAY, BUT several of us have been talking about it and you're doing too much. You're taking on things that don't need to be done by you, and you're letting families get away with doing too little to help their kin. Your time is better spent elsewhere."

White-haired and wrinkled, Mabel was gentle and kind, and I could tell she had thought for a long time about what to say. I also knew that it wasn't easy for her to confront me this directly. Her voice cracked slightly as she stopped to sip her tea. My cheeks flushed as I considered her gentle reprimand.

Doing too much. It was a struggle of mine. I wanted to go in and rescue people from their problems—make calls, round up support, act now. Sometimes my intervention worked well; other times I was doing a lot of work that other people could do. It was as though I wanted to prove what a good pastor I was by not turning down anything that was asked of me, no matter how ridiculous the request was.

One afternoon I found myself cleaning the house of an elderly couple that I had helped move into an assisted-living facility. As I filled trash bag after trash bag, Mabel's words came back to me. The couple had grandchildren and nephews who could take care of this. I didn't have to do this task myself. It is one thing to work beside your people, and another to help them ignore their responsibilities.

Mabel's gentle rebuke held two lessons for me, first in what she said and second in saying anything at all. I am thankful that she was willing to share her heart with me and to be used by God that afternoon. Carefully examine each criticism you receive as a pastor. Look at it carefully, and then bring it to God. Did the Lord lead someone, a faithful witness, to share this critique with you? Ask God to help you listen to your people and to hear the voice of the Spirit in their words. ❧

3

The day she threw out the pot roast

Good and upright is the LORD;
therefore he instructs sinners in the way.
He leads the humble in what is right,
and teaches the humble his way. . . .
For your name's sake, O LORD,
pardon my guilt, for it is great.

—PSALM 25:8–9,11

"I HAD A HOMEMADE POT ROAST WITH CARROTS AND POTATOES. Fresh bread. Lemon pound cake. A gallon of iced tea—sweetened, too, just the way you like it. I spent all day making everything. I stirred and looked out the window for you. I threw it out when I realized you weren't coming."

Speechless, I anchored the phone to my shoulder, grabbed for my calendar, and continued to listen to the woman's litany as I quickly flipped pages. There it was, in black and white—my commitment to stay with the older woman that day while her daughter, who was sixty-five herself, was having surgery at a hospital an hour away. My parishioner was nervous and afraid for her daughter, and she hadn't wanted to be alone in case a call came that something had gone wrong.

And I had blown it. Totally forgotten. I didn't have even a remotely good excuse, although I tried to think of one all the way over to her house. I even circled the block once trying to think of a better reason for my absence than, "I forgot." When I knocked on her front door, I was ready with a series of lame reasons I hadn't been there.

That is, I was ready until she opened the door. I was convicted by tear-stained cheeks and red, swollen eyes before I could say a word. I was guilty and I knew it. The crime was neglect, and I deserved whatever punishment she was going to dole out.

That was the first big mistake I made in my first pastorate. It was not, I confess, my last. I wish that I could say that I apologized profusely and that she forgave me immediately. I did apologize, both in person and in writing, but weeks passed before she would speak to me, and months slipped away before I was totally forgiven. I sensed that forgiveness when she handed me my Christmas present, a daily devotional, in June.

I watch my calendar more closely now, and I haven't missed an appointment since. But, I'm not perfect. Another mistake is lurking just around the corner. Even the most cautious pastors on occasion hurt people's feelings inadvertently. But if you are willing to accept responsibility and have the grace to apologize, the wounds you inflict don't have to be fatal to your relationships. There may still be a pot roast in my future—and this time, I won't miss it. ❧

How many cats can you bury?

Our God, you are the one
who rides on the clouds,
and we praise you.
Your name is the Lord—
and we celebrate
as we worship you.
Our God, from your sacred home
you take care of orphans
and protect widows.
You find families
for those who are lonely.

—Psalm 68:4–6, CEV

"You are not going to believe this," blurted my husband as soon as I walked in the door. I braced myself for the worst.

"Go ahead. I'm ready."

"Black cat died today." Behind him, I could hear the sad sniffles of our preschooler. This was our second feline death in as many weeks. How much could one family take?

"Where is he?" I asked, quietly pleased not to see any evidence of cat carnage on the living-room floor.

Overhearing my question, my daughter jumped up, her grief

temporarily forgotten. "We buried him next to Banana (our first cat casualty). It was so cool. Do you wanna go see?"

We walked across the field to a sunny spot under a small tree. We hadn't been at the church very long—just two summers. But that had been long enough for my daughter to learn how to ride her bike, to have her first day of school, and to say goodbye to two favorite pets. And it had been long enough to come to care about the people, to hurt when they hurt, to rejoice when they rejoiced.

We can approach being a pastor in a couple of ways. The easiest is to maintain a professional distance and to stay calm, cool, and collected. This approach views each pastorate as a step up the professional ladder. The next church is always slightly bigger, with more money, power, and prestige. The second way is a little more difficult. It says that wherever God sends us is home. That whomever God gives us to pastor is family. That whomever we are given, we love.

As a pastor, you will lead a unique life in a lot of ways. You may live in a home that does not belong to you; somebody else will pay the mortgage. Your pastorate may only last a few years before the moving van again comes calling. And yet, where God plants you, you are expected to grow . . . to set down roots, to plant seeds of relationship, to cultivate love and mercy, to bury strangers and friends—and cats. And for as long as God calls you to pastor among these people, this is where you belong. This is home. And that is enough.

Biding one's time

I am longing to see you so that I may share with you
some spiritual gift to strengthen you—or rather
so that we may be mutually encouraged by each other's faith,
both yours and mine.

—Romans 1:11–12

I hated that cat. Daisy was not only ugly; she wasn't very bright. I could not believe I had agreed to keep this cat. *Make mental note to check my job description,* I decided as I knelt on the cold garage floor, trying to tempt the animal out of the crawl space where she had taken up residence. Daisy had been a plea bargain. Daisy's mom, an eighty-seven-year-old woman who had fallen and been injured, would only agree to go to the rehabilitation center if I would take her cat. Daisy was the center of her life.

Temporarily dazed by the woman's unexpected capitulation, I agreed to her terms. After all, I had two other cats. How hard could one more be? Well, Daisy proved to be far more difficult than I could have ever imagined. She hid in the crawl space for a month, then outside for another five or six weeks. She came back only at night and then only to eat. Afraid for her safety outdoors, my husband decided to build an elaborate trap to catch her, a task that involved hours of work.

That afternoon, I was having lunch downtown with a member of my church who could best be described as a curmudgeon. Slow to please, he had a rather grumpy personality and always saw the glass as half empty. At the end of our lunch together, he added gruffly, "I want you to know that I pray for you. Every night before I go to sleep and I say my prayers, I always pray for you."

Who would've thought? His words and the prayers he confided were a good gift that I gladly received and treasured as a break-through that had been a long time in coming.

Meanwhile, at home, the trap was finished, my husband was tired, and he opened the door to go inside. As he did, Daisy strolled up, sniffed at the trap, and waltzed in the front door for the first time—as if she owned the place! After three months of hiding, she had been won over, by what we'll never know. And after two years of ministry, so was my curmudgeon friend. Two break-throughs in one day!

Getting to know your members and getting them to trust you can take time. Don't let your impatience ruin the opportunity to allow relationships to grow and develop. Pray for someone who seems difficult or frustrating. Ask for wisdom in showing God's love to them. ❧

I don't get paid enough

Let Israel be glad in its Maker; . . .
For the LORD takes pleasure in his people; . . .

—PSALM 149:2,4

I DON'T GET PAID ENOUGH MONEY TO DO THIS, I THOUGHT AS I valiantly attempted to assist the large, but somehow still frail, elderly woman. With one hand, I held an empty ice cream container so she could urinate into it. Moaning loudly and clutching her walker, she tried to stand. She had broken her arm earlier that day in a fall, and had been released from the hospital—bandaged, bruised, and unable to use one arm. Consequently, she had a very difficult time lifting herself up on the walker.

That's where I came in. When I handed her some toilet paper, she complained again: "That isn't enough paper for my cat, much less for me." Sighing, I went back to the bathroom, which had no running water and a cracked, filthy sink. I hesitated to touch anything without the benefit of gloves. I shuddered as a roach crawled across the bathtub.

Driving home much later, I became increasingly frustrated with family members who wouldn't take care of their own. I was also irritated with the woman's reluctance to accept any but the most minimal assistance. It was midnight before I pulled into my own driveway, tired and resentful.

A few days later, I stood by a hospital bed where a young mother and father introduced me to their long-awaited firstborn, a son. As I gingerly cradled the infant and stood with his parents, we were humbled by the miracle of new life. Out of that awe, we began to pray. We thanked God for their son and sought God's guidance for the part we would each play in his life. Feeling God's presence among us, we huddled together in a circle of love around the newborn.

I realized then that, if only I would look, I would see that I am paid well indeed. Thank God for the opportunities to be a part of such joy and wonder as well as for the times of difficulties and frustrations. There are blessings to be had in walking with our members through their highs *and* their lows. ❧

Who me?

Such is the confidence we have through Christ toward God. Not that we are competent of ourselves to claim anything as coming from us; our competence is from God, . . .

—2 CORINTHIANS 3:4–5

THE YOUNG WIDOW CRIED, PATTING HER INFANT DAUGHTER ON THE back. I stood by her husband's coffin and watched as her parents and his numbly filed into the seats around her. Dozens of family members and friends huddled under umbrellas around the canopy as the rain drizzled on the dark, somber morning.

As the funeral director nodded to signal that it was time to begin the service, my heart clenched with a cold fear. What could I possibly say? My notes, stained by raindrops, seemed worthless now. What could I possibly offer that could make a difference here? These people needed someone more wise, more spiritually mature, someone more . . . than me.

As pastors, we are humbled to stand before a family and commit their loved ones to God, to watch as they caress the lid of a closed casket before they walk away, with heads hung low. To meet their eyes, to offer a word of solace is *hard.*

That rain-drenched day I realized that on my own strength, I cannot do it. The task is simply too difficult. But today, as I look into the eyes of waiting parents and spouses and children, I am reminded of Christ's sufficiency. He is stronger than I am. He is more wise than I, more compassionate. And he loves these people much more than I ever could.

Pastors are called to do difficult and emotionally draining jobs, tasks that require a source of strength beyond our own. We are quick to offer Jesus to our congregation, but slower to accept him and his strength for ourselves, to give up our own independence and lean on him. Pray that you would depend on Christ today. ❧

Gather 'round

. . . whoever wishes to be great among you must be your servant,
. . . just as the Son of Man came not to be served but to serve,
and to give his life a ransom for many.

—MATTHEW 20:26,28

"IT'S A PRISON, REALLY," EXPLAINS THE SMALL, ALMOST DAINTY, ninety-seven-year-old woman. She is describing her new home, an apartment in a posh, assisted-living facility, that she shares with her husband of seventy-six years. "It is a very nice prison, but a prison nevertheless." She sighs and looks out the window across a field of tall, golden stalks of corn.

"Tell me what it was like during your first winter in North Dakota," I urge, getting settled on her faded, chintz-covered couch. "We left off last time where you had just met the Russian immigrants who were going to be your students." Amazingly, her mind, under attack from dementia and fuzzy on the best days, brought back clear memories of years earlier.

Her gray eyes sparkled as she regaled me with tale after tale of her experiences of being a seventeen-year-old, Midwestern girl sent to North Dakota all alone to teach immigrant children who knew no English. She told of mischievous students, a mean landlady, and harsh winters. I wished that her great-grandchildren were around to hear the stories as well. She loved to tell them.

Listening to the elderly woman tell stories I had already heard a dozen times before was the most important ministry I had done all week. "The next time you come," she promised, "I will tell you all about when I first met Henry."

As I rose to say good-bye, I smiled and said honestly, "I will look forward to it."

As pastors, we need to hear our people's stories, to understand their past, and to invite them to reflect on and share their memories. *Pray* for those who are alone, and look for ways to draw out the stories from some of the people you visit this week, especially the elderly. Those visits are among the most meaningful and important visits you can make. ❧

9

Do the right thing

Then you will understand righteousness and justice
and equity, every good path;
for wisdom will come into your heart,
and knowledge will be pleasant to your soul;
prudence will watch over you;
and understanding will guard you.

—PROVERBS 2:9–11

THE TELEPHONE STARTED RINGING EARLY AND IT RANG FREQUENTLY. Only a few days were needed for word to get out that I had made someone angry enough to leave the church—to walk out in the middle of service, in fact. The woman, who had been a faithful member for years, was furious over a decision I had made that affected someone in her family.

This was the first time I had ever had someone leave the church because of something I had done. It was not an accomplishment of which I was proud, and the days and weeks following the member's withdrawal were not an easy time. A good many people in the congregation were watching me as an individual leader and us as a church during that period, watching to see if their church stood by what we said it did. They watched to see if we could offer love and grace and still stand firm by what was right. The family has not yet returned. But every once in awhile, some of the members call them and let them know we miss them, that we are praying for them and hoping that all is well.

All pastors, at one time or another in our ministries, cause some offense that results in a break in relationship. Regardless of with whom the fault lies and whether the offense is personal or principled, people within and beyond the church are paying close attention to how we, as leaders, will handle the conflict. We have a responsibility to act according to Christ's love and God's Word, to reconcile brokenness whenever possible without compromising our faith and integrity.

Seek God's wisdom and courage to make a stand when necessary to do so in your ministry. Pray for God's love and grace to shine through every decision you make in your pastorate, and ask the Spirit to mediate the conflict through you and to heal the broken relationships in your congregation and community. ❧

Light in the darkness

In the beginning was the Word, and the Word was with God,
and the Word was God. He was in the beginning with God.
All things came into being through him, and without him
not one thing came into being. What has come
into being in him was life, and the life was the light
of all people. The light shines in the darkness,
and the darkness did not overcome it.

—JOHN 1:1–5

THIS WAS NOT YOUR TRADITIONAL CHRISTMAS EVE SERVICE. THE sanctuary looked the same, the poinsettia were in place, and we sang all the same hymns, but the congregation had changed since last Christmas. The year had been a tough one; we felt a little banged and bruised. Too many deaths, too many losses. How could we avoid thinking about empty places in the pews and the empty chairs around tomorrow's dinner table? In a lot of ways, we were glad to get the year behind us.

Out of the silence, an older widower walked slowly to the podium. I couldn't imagine how he felt, spending his first Christmas in sixty years without his spouse. He cleared his throat and spoke a few words. He said that God is good and that he was trusting in the Lord. The next man who spoke talked about losing a son-in-law too soon. His voice broke as he, too, acknowledged that God is good and that he was confident God was still at work in the lives of his family members.

As the service ended, the congregation moved of its own accord out of the pews and into a circle, each person holding a small, white candle. I watched the shadows flicker as, one by one, the candles were lit. The room, filled with darkness moments earlier, was aglow with light. Yes, the year had been hard, but our little community had come together to proclaim that God was still on the throne and that they still believed in God's promises. Their testimony proved that light still shines in dark places.

When pastors are able to truly worship and not just orchestrate a service, we are indeed blessed. We need such opportunities to be refreshed and strengthened for our journey. As you plan and prepare for the services at your church, pray that you don't lose the sense of holy awe when you feel the presence of God in worship. ❧

11

Once upon a time

Church officials must be in control of their
own families, and they must see that
their children are obedient and always respectful.
If they don't know how to control their own families,
how can they look after God's people?

—1 TIMOTHY 3:4–5, CEV

"ONCE UPON A TIME, IN A FARAWAY PLACE, IN A FARAWAY LAND, THERE was a beautiful princess—" My daughter tensed as the phone rang. Before the second ring had finished, she had already slipped from my lap. She knew that, invariably, a telephone call meant a fifteen-minute or more conversation and that, at least for now, our story time was over.

My heart sank at her immediate response. I felt such guilt that she sensed who was more important to me at that time. Then and there I decided that she should be able to hear the rest of her story read without being tossed aside by the phone. "It's OK, honey," I said. "We're going to let it ring." With a big smile, she jumped back up into my lap and snuggled even closer.

In fact, that precedent became a new rule at our house. If you are reading a story to our daughter, you can't answer the phone. Family comes first. The decision was a matter of establishing our priorities.

As pastors, we often struggle with balancing the needs of our families against the demands of our churches. We must remember that God wants us to take care of our families. We ourselves need the opportunity to be strengthened by our families, and they need our love and support.

Ask God to help you create the boundaries you need so that you can honor your family time. Pray for the ability to set reasonable limits on your availability to your members. Your family deserves to know that—excepting extreme emergencies—they have you all to themselves, at least part of the time. ❧

Learning to listen

I regard everything as loss because of the surpassing value of knowing Christ Jesus my Lord. . . .

—PHILIPPIANS 3:8

QUIETLY OPENING THE DOOR, I WHISPERED HER NAME. THERE WAS NO response other than the drip of the IV tube and the hum of the oxygen machine. Seeing that Vivienne was resting comfortably, I closed the door. Checking with the nurse at the front desk, I asked about the status of the patient, an elderly church member who had been admitted for pneumonia. To my surprise, the nurse said Vivienne's condition had improved dramatically and that she would be going back to the nursing home within a few days.

At the elevator doors, I checked my watch, pleased that, since the woman had been sleeping, I had an extra half an hour in my jam-packed day. Now I could fit in another visit before lunch. As I stepped into the elevator, I reached for my day-planner, looking for the next name on my list. And then I stopped. I felt called to go back to Vivienne's room. *That's ridiculous,* I told myself. *She's fine. I don't want to disturb her.* I had to admit, though, that part of my reluctance arose from the pressure of my busy schedule. Still, I felt clearly that I needed to go back to her room and pray with her.

Not wanting to argue with what I knew was God's leading, I stepped back out of the elevator and walked back down the hallway. The nurse with whom I had just spoken was just leaving Vivienne's room. "Forget something?" the nurse asked.

"Yes, I did." When I entered the room this time, I sat down, removed my jacket, and took out my Bible. While Vivienne slept, I read to her. I shared familiar passages that offered comfort and solace. And then I prayed. While I was not sure how aware she was of my presence, I had the sense that she was conscious on some level. As I prayed with her, the Spirit led me to talk about preparing for death and accepting God's love and grace. It was not my usual bedside prayer.

I was not at all surprised, then, to learn later that Vivienne died that night in her sleep. Being open to God's leading and direction during pastoral calls can make all the difference—to the people with whom we visit and to we ourselves. Ask God to be with you and to direct your words and prayers as you spend time with those under your care. ❧

13

Lifted up

But Moses' hands grew weary;
so they took a stone and put it under him,
and he sat on it. Aaron and Hur held up his hands,
one on one side, and the other on the other side;
so his hands were steady until the sun set.

—Exodus 17:12

The blank computer screen taunted me. Struggling to keep my eyes open, I tried to focus on my sermon. The task seemed impossible. I checked my watch, noting I had only about fifteen hours before I had to preach. I could barely conceive that just two days earlier I had been printing out my finished sermon when the telephone had rung.

A young dad, just twenty-nine years old, had not made it to work that day, the victim of a confused elderly driver. I was up late that night, praying and thinking about the man's services. By the time I had fallen asleep, it was past one in the morning. Unbelievably, by three, the phone had rung again. This time, a thirty-two-year-old father had died in his sleep. His was the sixth death in as many weeks for our small church. It seemed like a nightmare that wouldn't stop. How much more could we take?

And so I found myself on Saturday afternoon, rewriting my sermon. Or I would have been had I any idea what to say—or just a few more hours of sleep. I knew my sermon had to address the twin shocks our church had just faced, and yet I struggled with where to begin. As I made random notes, I heard a knock on the door. Relieved by the reprieve, I was surprised to see an older couple standing there, members of the congregation. They had come to let me know they were thinking about me and to pray with me as I prepared my sermon. We held hands as they ministered to me through their prayers.

When they left, the phone rang. This time another member was calling, wanting me to know that he, too, was praying for me. I was touched by the thoughtfulness and willingness of my members to be used by God. Bowing my head, I thanked God for showing such compassionate care through my people.

The sermon came. God had provided an "Aaron" for me that day—people who held up my hands so that I could minister when I simply could not do it otherwise. More than once, my people have been a precious gift. As pastors, we are tempted to carry the burden of all our folk on our shoulders. Sometimes we forget that even as God has given them into our care, they are also given to us as support and encouragement in *our* times of need. May God help you always to receive such an offering.

14

Sunday's comin'!

When I came to you, brothers and sisters,
I did not come proclaiming the mystery of God
to you in lofty words or wisdom. For I decided
to know nothing among you except Jesus Christ,
and him crucified. And I came to you in weakness
and in fear and in much trembling. My speech
and my proclamation were not with plausible words
of wisdom, but with a demonstration of the Spirit
and of power, so that your faith might rest not on
human wisdom but on the power of God.

—1 Corinthians 2:1–5

Perhaps I should have gone to medical school. At least then I wouldn't have to make a fool out of myself in front of a hundred people every Sunday, I mused as I smiled and nodded, shaking everyone's hand as the congregation left. I wondered just how much oxygen I had wasted during my twenty-minute sermon that morning. Quite possibly it had been one of the worst messages I had ever preached.

I went home incredibly discouraged. My husband vainly attempted to help, saying, "Well, I'm sure that people appreciated the effort." He only confirmed that the sermon had gone as badly as I feared. I wanted to crawl under a rock and feel sorry for myself. Perhaps I had misunderstood God's call. Perhaps I wasn't really supposed to be doing this after all. My pity party lasted all afternoon.

Preaching every week is a difficult task. Some Sunday mornings all the stars seem to line up. Our illustrations sparkle, and our points are clear, concise, and captivating. And then there are those *other* Sundays.

Every once in a while, every pastor bombs. It happens to the best of us. The reasons vary. Sometimes, we aren't adequately prepared; we haven't spend enough time in the Word; we haven't struggled with the text, sought God's voice, sweated over it. Sometimes, we just don't have enough time for that kind of struggle.

But some weeks, the best efforts in the world just fall flat, and the sermon just doesn't come together. Don't despair. No one expects flawless sermons week after week—no one except you, of course! But, another Sunday is always just around the corner.

Seek God as you prepare your sermon this week. Are you taking the time to really listen to what the Spirit is telling you? Wait upon the Lord and allow God to speak through your message.

15

God's day-planner

O God, you are my God, I seek you,
my soul thirsts for you;
my flesh faints for you,
as in a dry and weary land where there is no water.
So I have looked upon you in the sanctuary,
beholding your power and glory.
Because your steadfast love is better than life,
my lips will praise you.

—PSALM 63:1–3

MY TO-DO LIST FOR THE DAY WAS LONG: CALL THE PEST CONTROL people and tell them about the mice in the attic; argue with the photocopier people about replacing the lemon they sent the church; pick up office supplies downtown. Sandwiched in there were a few pastoral calls as well as a quick review of the Bible study lesson for tomorrow.

I have found that the rhythm of my days is different somehow than what I expected while sitting in my seminary classroom. Then I envisioned long, quiet, uninterrupted hours of study and reflection in anticipation of the following week's sermon, followed by an afternoon of pastoral calls and one or two evenings a week taken with church activities. I didn't realize that opportunities for quiet mornings of study are rare, that pastoral calls happen at all hours of the day and night, and that committee meetings have been known to last longer than the Israelites' sojourn in the wilderness.

As pastors, we need to learn the wisdom of starting the day off quietly, spending time with the Lord, and then listing the most urgent things that needed to get done that day. Fill in around the edges with the extras. Say "no" to activities in the community and in the denomination if saying "yes" means feeling rushed and out of control. Not everything is a priority.

Spend time with God every morning before deciding the business of the day. After all, who is in charge of your schedule? Create enough margin in your schedule to be open to God. Leave room in your day-planner for God to surprise you.

Snow, ice, and contentment

Always be joyful and never stop praying.
Whatever happens, keep thanking God because of
Jesus Christ. That is what God wants you to do.

—1 THESSALONIANS 5:16–18, CEV

I SHIVERED AS ANOTHER COLD GUST OF WIND RATTLED THE WINDOWS. The winter blast had brought sixteen inches of snow to our community, more than I had ever seen at one time. The wind chill was 15 degrees below zero, colder than I had ever experienced before as well. I don't like snow, ice, or sleet. Being a native of Virginia, I missed the warmth of my home state! Moving farther north was not an easy transition for me.

In fact, I had a laundry list of complaints about our new place of residence: the schools weren't great; the town seemed bleak; the newspaper was horrible, to name just a few. I scanned the want ads in journals occasionally, sometimes stopping at a job description that seemed perfect. *Now I would be happy with this,* I would think wistfully as I dog-eared the page.

One morning, I found a job posting that seemed perfect for me—it was everything I wanted. My husband encouraged me to apply, and I said I would. Although I admitted that I should probably pray about it first, I hesitated to do so because I was pretty sure that God wasn't finished using me where I was. I was not surprised then, when God's message was clear: "You can't be released from here until you learn to be happy where you are. A church needs a pastor who is content."

That wasn't what I wanted to hear—but it was what I needed. My rebellious attitude was keeping me from adjusting to our new home. Snow or no snow, this was where I had been called to pastor, and this was where I had committed to make my home, weather not withstanding.

As pastors, we may not be serving where we planned to serve or even doing what we expected to do, but we need to decide in what we place our trust—in our own plans or in God's? Do we truly trust God for our ministry?

Check your attitude. Guard against a rebellious spirit that would separate you from closeness with the Lord. Seek God's contentment. ☙

17

A child alone

He called a child, whom he put among them, and said, "Truly I tell you, unless you change and become like children, you will never enter the kingdom of heaven. Whoever becomes humble like this child is the greatest in the kingdom of heaven. Whoever welcomes one such child in my name welcomes me."

—MATTHEW 18:2–5

I AM NOT A SUPERSTITIOUS PERSON, BUT I HAD AN UNEASY FEELING that the black cat on my front porch was not a good sign. I recognized the cat; it belonged to a twelve-year-old girl down the street. Dawn came to church by herself, riding her bicycle and looking sort of forlorn. Rarely was she dressed warmly enough, and she always ate ravenously when she was offered food.

She came to a few youth events, and I tried to get to know her. Our local school was her fifth of the year, and Christmas had not even arrived yet. Obviously, there were some serious problems in her family. As I spent time with her, bits and pieces of her story began to come out. I agonized over how best to help her. I talked with social services, but although they admitted Dawn's was an unfortunate situation, they didn't have enough evidence to get involved yet.

One cold Sunday evening, I looked out the window at the drizzly weather, thankful for the warmth inside. Then I saw

Dawn, huddled against the cold, protected only by a thin dress. I invited her in, fixed hot cocoa and sandwiches, and we began to talk. She opened up to me that night, beginning to share some of the horror of her family life. What she confided wasn't enough to have her removed immediately, but I thought social services would be able to act. I tried to convince Dawn not to go home until we got someone to help, but she wanted to get her brother out first.

So, when I opened the door the next morning and saw the black cat sitting on the porch, I knew it wasn't a good sign. I went over to the house quickly, but I was too late. The family was gone. The mother and boyfriend had left in the night, loading their car, taking Dawn and her brother with them.

I was heartbroken. I felt guilty for not doing more and found myself second-guessing everything I had done. I thought about Dawn for months, praying that she would find her voice again and keep using it until someone else heard her and got her the help she needed.

Every pastor is faced with those times when we need to act to protect a child. Many times, we feel helpless and even hopeless in the face of their pain. Ask God's protection over the children in your congregation and community, and at the same time, make yourself aware of the resources available to help families in trouble. Pray for sensitivity toward the needs of the children with whom you have contact. ❧

Lessons to be learned

You have often heard me teach. Now I want you to tell these same things to followers who can be trusted to tell others.

—2 Timothy 2:2, CEV

After her last round of chemotherapy, Tanya's tests showed that she was in remission again. "Then they told me I only have a 20 percent chance of living ten years. I laughed at them," said Tanya, a twenty-nine-year-old wife and mother of three. "They must not know me very well. I've beaten cancer three times already. This is just another bump in the road."

Tanya was amazing to me—and everyone else who has met her. *Here is someone,* I marveled, *only a few months younger than me, who has looked death squarely in the eyes and laughed.* She appeared so vibrant and alive, I couldn't imagine her body being attacked by cancer. Her concern was not for her own life, but for her children and how much they needed her.

I was humbled as she left my office that night. The irritations in my life had loomed so large just a few hours earlier. They paled now in comparison with what Tanya was facing. *If spending time with her doesn't put things in perspective, nothing will,* I told myself. I admired her grace. I was awed by her strength, her courage, and her willingness to keep fighting. I have been blessed to sit under such a wise teacher.

As pastors, we encounter an incredible array of traumas, dysfunctions, and heartbreaks. Sometimes, hidden in the rubble of sin and misfortune is a gem: a life well lived and strength, determination, and faith in the face of adversity. Don't close yourself off to learning life lessons from your members. They, like Tanya, have a lot to teach. ☙

19

The big question

God's ways are as mysterious as the pathway of the wind, and as the manner in which a human spirit is infused into the little body of a baby while it is yet in its mother's womb.

—Ecclesiastes 11:5, TLB

I wasn't surprised when the call came. We all knew that Tanya was living on borrowed time. Still, we had thought she would have a while longer before the cancer reared its head again. Only a few months had passed since her last treatment, and the cancer was already back, this time in her liver. The disease was inoperable. Chemotherapy would buy her some time, but no one knew just how long.

As is common among people who suffer a tremendous loss or shock, Tanya—the same optimistic young woman who had laughed at her 20 percent chance of living ten years—wanted to know why. It is the million dollar question for pastors. We get asked "why?" so many times—beside hospital beds and coffins, after doctor's appointments and test results. "Why me?" "Why her?" "There are a thousand people who deserved this more than he did." "What did I do wrong?" All people want to make sense out of senseless tragedies. That desire is a part of who we are as human beings. We want the world to be just and fair. For the most part, we think we ought to get what we deserve.

So, pastors have the difficult task of looking at people who have had their lives ripped to shreds and saying, "I don't know. I agree with you completely. This does not make any sense. I cannot begin to understand it. But God is still here. And I do know that God loves you and cares for you and wants to help you walk through this."

Pray for your people who are going through a difficult time right now. Maybe they have lost their own health or independence, or perhaps someone they love has died. Pray for a spirit of peace and comfort that will endure with them through the coming weeks and months. ❧

20

Close to home

So we can say with confidence,
"The Lord is my helper;
I will not be afraid.
What can anyone do to me?"
—HEBREWS 13:6

I HAVE NEVER MINDED VISITING HOSPITALS. PRISONS—MEN'S PRISONS—however, are another story. Quite frankly, they terrify me. I can almost hear my heart pounding when I enter the building. I go when I have to, but I don't like it. Dealing with manipulative or angry men takes me back to being abused as a child, and I am uncomfortable in such men's company. While much healing has taken place in my life, I am just not the best pastor for those folks.

Too often, pastors don't want to admit that we struggle sometimes. We don't want to admit that we aren't always all together. But the best pastors are the ones who can look at certain situations honestly and recognize how those circumstances effect them. In some situations, a pastor needs to say, "I want to help you get the help you need, but I am not the right person to help you. Here are some other possibilities." In other situations, just having an awareness of how personal history has an impact on the pastoral role is enough.

Having someone to talk with helps immensely. A good friend is a tremendous blessing. A mentor, someone who is older and wiser, is even better. Many pastors benefit from a peer support group whose members help one another seriously examine such concerns. We need to be aware of our emotional struggles, so that we can continue to work through them and seek God's healing.

Examine your life experiences and consider how those experiences have influenced your ability to minister in particular situations or to certain people. Identify those situations in which you find it difficult to serve, and assess why that is. What kind of support system do you have in place for dealing with these concerns? Is it adequate? Ask God to reveal where you need to grow and when you need to exercise discernment.

21

Made by hand

Make a joyful noise to the L*ORD, all the earth!*
Worship the L*ORD with gladness;*
come into his presence with singing.
Know that the L*ORD is God!*
It is he that made us, and we are his;
we are his people, and the sheep of his pasture.

—PSALM 100:1–3

I HAD ACCEPTED MY FIRST PASTORATE ONLY A FEW MONTHS AGO, AND things were going well. In fact, they were going great. I had just finished an afternoon of visitation, and the calls had gone smoothly. This was surprising because only a few months earlier I had been terrified trying to think of something to say to all the people I had to visit. Having conversations with virtual strangers was not easy for me. But once I had gotten started, I found that I loved the chance to be with the people in the congregation and get to know them better.

Coming home, I thanked God for a good afternoon of visitation, for the opportunity to start building relationships. I found myself thinking, *I have such the right job for me. It's as if I was made to do this.* Slowly, the mental lightbulb came on. God *had,* in fact, created me to do just this. When I was still in my mother's womb, God was planning my ministry. Those whom

God has called, God has also prepared. The Lord has given the skills, talents, and abilities to do the task at hand.

As pastors, we should try to remember that on days when we feel less than adequate, when we are not sure if we have what it takes to do what we have been asked to do. God *wants* us to be in this place. *This* is where God has placed us. This calling is not a mistake or an accident. And if we believe that, then we must also believe that God knows what we need to accomplish what we have been called to do.

Spend some time thanking God for the abilities you have been given to develop for ministry. How has God blessed you? Lift up to God any doubts or concerns you have about your abilities. ❧

22

Great expectations

Why am I discouraged?
Why am I restless?
I trust you!
And I will praise you again
because you help me,
and you are my God.

—Psalm 42:5, CEV

The volunteer sign-up sheet is empty again. Someone's feelings have been hurt by another's thoughtless remarks. Someone else agrees to head up a project, and then they let it fall apart. A project is supported by just a few faithful members, but they are the same ones who seem to do everything.

When the members of our churches let us down, the disappointment isn't easy to take. We wish that they would act more kind and faithfully. Sometimes, their lack of follow-through makes us look bad. Other times, we are stuck cleaning up the consequences of someone else's actions. *If only* . . . We know the church could be a better place to be, if only. . . .

You know what I mean. After all, this is your life. You have sacrificed a lot to pastor where you are. You eat, sleep, and breathe the church. Not a day goes by that you don't think about the church and its members—even while you are on vacation. It seems inconceivable that the members would not care as much as you do.

Some *do* care, but they don't have the time, energy, or resources to do any more. Others are so hungry for what the church offers to them that they aren't ready to give back. Still others love the church, but they don't realize that their actions—or inactions—create problems. Only a very few folks are so unhealthy that they intentionally inflict distress—and they need to be in the church as much as (or more than!) anyone else.

Go to God and ask the Spirit to help you examine your expectations for your church and its people. Are those expectations too lofty for right now? Are your goals reasonable for what your people have to give? Don't try to fill in the gaps you perceive. Doing so robs them of their responsibility. Don't resent those who let you down; forgive them. Hold them accountable when you need to, but accept them—flaws and all. They are, after all, the flock that God has given to you.

23

Green-eyed monsters

No, dear brothers and sisters, I am still not all I should be,
but I am focusing all my energies on this one thing:
Forgetting the past and looking forward to what lies ahead,
I strain to reach the end of the race and receive the prize
for which God, through Christ Jesus, is calling us up to heaven.

—PHILIPPIANS 3:13–14, NLT

ALL RIGHT, I CONFESS. I WAS SECRETLY RELIEVED WHEN I HEARD THAT a neighboring pastor had been asked to resign. I had been reading about his accomplishments for months in the denominational newsletter, all the while making comparisons between our ministries. It was painfully obvious that he was doing much more with his church than I was accomplishing at mine. I was so jealous I couldn't stand it. Were his people better? Did they have more resources? Or—and I hated to even consider the possibility—was he just a better pastor than I?

Not that I wanted to be the best pastor in the denomination; I just was afraid of not doing *well.* I didn't want to be the kind of pastor who moves from one church to another every three years because nobody wants to keep him or her. And I figured that as long as other pastors were doing more poorly than I was, then surely that was enough to keep the moving van at bay for me.

As pastors, we don't like to admit that sometimes we feel jealous. We know the feeling is beneath us, yet we still compare our church growth and successes with that of our friends who started pastoring at the same time. We know better than to play the number game and brag about how many folks are warming our pews, but we do. We even read denominational magazines and church-growth books that highlight pastors who double and triple their congregations in just a few years—never mind that, for most pastors of small churches, every new person who walks through the doors and *stays* is something of a miracle. Very few of us have the sort of charismatic zeal that will build a megachurch. But if we're honest, we confess that sometimes we sure would like to!

Examine your heart before the Lord, and ask God to root out any jealous feelings you might be harboring. Seek to get rid of a competitive spirit. Invite God to be the judge of your success as a pastor. Remind yourself that, in the end, it is your faithfulness to our Lord that matters most.

24

The pressure's on

And now a word to you parents. Don't keep on scolding and nagging your children, making them angry and resentful. Rather, bring them up with the loving discipline the Lord himself approves, with suggestions and godly advice.

—EPHESIANS 6:4, TLB

SHE HAD BEEN REMINDED REPEATEDLY TO *WALK* DOWN THE AISLE FOR children's message. Usually, the towheaded little girl forgot as soon as her feet touched the runner. In short order, she skipped, hopped, and sometimes ran toward the front, much to her pastoral parent's chagrin and the congregation's amusement. Finally, in desperation, the father threatened to withhold the privilege of children's church if she ran down the aisle again.

Head bowed in disappointment, she nodded and began walking up the aisle. She walked slowly and deliberately, as if she were a flower girl in a wedding. Her father smiled and nodded at her mother, who was watching from a seat behind the pulpit. Amazed, the mother was impressed with the father's negotiating tactics as their daughter neared the front.

As she came within just a few feet of the gathered group of children, her parents breathed a sigh of relief. Finally, she had shown everyone that she could act appropriately. And just then, so quickly you almost missed it if you weren't looking, Kaylyn did a beautiful somersault, ending with outstretched arms and a loud, "Ta-daaah!"

My daughter—pastor's kid and resident acrobat.

Pastors' families—especially the children, or "PKs" as they are sometimes known—don't have an easy time, in church or out of it. While many clergy talk about the expectations that church members have about how their children and spouse should act, my experience has been different. I have found that my own expectations, especially for my daughter, were higher than anyone else's could have been. For the first several months of my pastorate, I was too harsh with her and expected too much. Because I wanted people to think I was a good parent, I wanted my child's behavior to be perfect. I have mellowed some, but unreasonable expectations are always a concern.

What expectations do you have for your spouse and children? Are they fair? Examine them with your family and with God. Seek God's help to be a faithful parent and spouse.

Failure 101

But this made us stop trusting in ourselves and start trusting God, who raises the dead to life.

—2 CORINTHIANS 1:9, CEV

MY LATEST IDEA WAS SUCH A GOOD ONE! I JUST KNEW IT WAS THE thing that would turn the church around. My last few brainstorms had gone so smoothly that everyone approved this one quickly. Not only had I read about it in one of my pastors' magazines; I had heard about another pastor doing the same thing, and his attendance doubled in only a month—or something like that. I didn't bother with all the details; I was too excited about getting started.

Of course the idea, once implemented, flopped. And it didn't just fail; it failed miserably. Less than half a dozen people showed up for this great new programming idea, and the leader and I were two of the people present. I wanted to crawl under a rock. This was not one of my shining moments as a new pastor. I was so sure the idea would work, and I was so *embarrassed* when it didn't.

In a church, we pastors have fifty or seventy-five or one hundred people judging us on our ideas. That can be a tough crowd to please. And we feel absolutely humiliated when we blow it. But, perhaps those failures are an opportunity for God to remind us who is ultimately responsible for our churches—a not-so-subtle reminder that even our best ideas are no competition for a congregation that earnestly seeks the heart of God for their future.

Spend some time praying and putting your church under the sovereignty of God. What does God desire for your congregation? What does God want to accomplish? Are your goals and dreams aligned with your Lord's? ❧

26

More than 9 to 5

Unless the Lord *builds the house,*
those who build it labor in vain.
Unless the Lord *guards the city,*
the guard keeps watch in vain.
It is in vain that you rise up early
and go late to rest,
eating the bread of anxious toil;
for he gives sleep to his beloved.

—Psalm 127:1–2

Some days I need to be left absolutely alone by members of my congregation. Not that I don't love them or that I don't want to be a part of what is happening with them, but every once in a while, I just need space. I need my days off to be just that—off. I need days when I can turn the church off for twenty-four hours and not be needed in the middle of whatever it is I'm doing.

In so many ways, being a pastor to the people of God is a wonderful experience. But the feeling of being owned twenty-four hours a day, seven days a week can sometimes be overwhelming. Of course we know the elderly shut-in is lonely and likes to call "just to talk" a few times a week, and usually we don't mind—but sometimes we do! And we understand that questions about important church business will inevitably arise—"So sorry to bother you on your day off, but it will only take a minute . . ."—but rarely are the problems something that couldn't wait a day or two.

You can handle the practical aspects of establishing a true day off in several different ways—by leaving your answering machine on and reminding your folks about your scheduled off-days, for example. However, for me, the issue is about the general expectations of church members. If you are a private person like I am, intrusions can feel overbearing. I have to guard against feeling resentful toward those who need me when the time isn't convenient. That isn't the attitude that God wants me to have. Feelings of resentment separate me from God's people.

Do you also struggle with a spirit of resentment or irritability in the face of your members' demands? Do you just crave some down-time, a few precious hours alone with your own thoughts? Ask God to give you a loving spirit toward your needy flock, but pray also for opportunities to set aside time for yourself—and for the wisdom to take advantage of those opportunities, even when other concerns clamor for your attention. Seek the Spirit's reminder that without God's rest, we labor in vain.

27

A time to speak

So then, each of us will be accountable to God. Let us therefore no longer pass judgment on one another, but resolve instead never to put a stumbling block or hindrance in the way of another.

—Romans 14:12–13

"They say death always comes in threes," explained the older woman.

"Surely you don't think there will be another death, do you?" I asked incredulously. "We have had five deaths in as many weeks. How much worse could it be? Besides," I pointed out, "we've already had our third death."

She looked at me as if I couldn't count. "It starts over again. Didn't you know?" She shook her head. "I just wonder who it will be."

Seeing myself as a bearer of light into darkness, I tried to explain how superstitions were just that and there was no need to worry. She nodded politely and ignored me completely. "Comes in threes, you just wait and see," she said. "That's what my mama used to say and her mama before her." She shook her head at my youthful naivete and stubbornness. I left the house wondering how anyone in the twentieth century could believe in such an old wives' tale.

That very night, that woman's grandson died in his sleep from an illness no one had known about. *Comes in threes, indeed.* Our conversation came back to me as I sat in her living room early the next morning. In the larger scheme of things, did it matter if she believed an old wives' tale? Probably not. What mattered was whether she believed the gospel. I wished that I had spent less time debating the validity of a superstition and more time addressing the anxiety she obviously felt.

Just because we have an opinion doesn't mean that we, as pastors, have to share it. What a bitter pill to swallow—because we have so many good opinions! Yet as I discovered for myself, getting into discussions and even arguments about things that are eternally irrelevant may hinder us when we try to present the gospel.

Pray that the Lord would guide you in your discussions with your members. May you enjoy your time with them, learn to read between the lines of conversation, and discern when to be silent and when to speak. ❧

28

Living-room fellowship

If then there is any encouragement in Christ,
any consolation from love, any sharing in the Spirit,
any compassion and sympathy, make my joy complete:
be of the same mind, having the same love,
being in full accord and of one mind.

—PHILIPPIANS 2:1–2

"WHEN I COME HOME FROM SCHOOL, I HAVE A HARD TIME NOT treating Dwain like a first grader," explained a young wife and schoolteacher. "I'm still in that mode. So I will ask him, 'Are you sure that was the right decision to make?'" Dwain blushed, and the rest of us laughed as we remembered our own newlywed days.

As the steaming cups of coffee were slowly sipped, the atmosphere in the living room warmed. Bibles were opened in anticipation of the evening's study and discussion, and I was reminded of the early church as we gathered around on those couches and love seats and sought God together. It is an incredible experience when a small group gets together and commits to carve more time out of tightly packed schedules. I love to watch as my people come to know one another and begin to open up more fully and honestly with one another.

Some of the best moments in pastoral ministry can happen in small Bible studies in our members' living rooms. As participants pray for each other and reach out to one another, we can see God at work building those relationships. Bible studies such as these are not only an effective ministry; they offer the opportunity for pastor and members alike to share themselves. Each one of our stories is important, and living-room gatherings are ideal for cultivating real relationships and enjoying good, old-fashioned fellowship.

Take time now to pray for the small groups, if any, that are meeting in your church. If there are none, ask God to reveal to you if that is a ministry you should develop in your congregation.

29

A sloth comes to call

So teach us to count our days
that we may gain a wise heart.
—Psalm 90:12

"I sure wish I had your job, Pastor. Get a house to live in, utilities paid, too, and all you have to do is show up on Sunday mornings. Don't get much better than that!" I smiled politely as I tried to pretend that I hadn't heard that joke a million times before. I don't find it much funnier the more frequently I hear it, either. Like most pastors, I have typically put in a good forty-hour work week and then some.

But there have been times, I hate to admit, that I haven't worked as much as I should have. Sometimes pastors get lazy. We find that no one is around to see what we do all day, so our schedule is ours to create. At times, the freedom can be overwhelming. Although many pastors struggle with this, few of us want to admit it.

As long as we show up for all the right meetings and hospital visits, we can be tempted to slack off. What does it really matter if we're not at the office by 9:00 A.M.? Ten or eleven o'clock seems more reasonable, anyhow. And what's an extra day or two off a week? Does anybody really care? The problem is that laziness is often addictive. A few days of slothfulness can easily stretch into a few weeks, a few months, and finally, into a way of ministry—or not doing ministry, as the case may be.

Closely examine your work ethic. Are you prone to trying to get by with the least amount of effort? Is this a pattern you see repeated in your ministry? Keep a log of your hours to assess your fruitfulness. Ask God to give you the energy and motivation you need to be a good steward of your days. ☙

30

Cloud nine

Let the favor of the Lord our God be upon us,
and prosper for us the work of our hands—
O prosper the work of our hands!

—Psalm 90:17

I was on cloud nine. Finally—I had planned a successful event! At the risk of sounding arrogant, the program wasn't just marginally successful; it was *fantastic!* The pews were tightly packed; at least a dozen new faces were present; and the ushers were filing people into folding chairs in the back, the space usually reserved for Christmas and Easter services. A contagious spirit of excitement filled the air. After months of planning, we had finally pulled it off. This was my first real success at my new church, and it felt *great.*

As pastors, such exhilarating highs can be few and far between. The sad fact is that no matter what wonderful thing we do, someone in the church will find fault with it. New people in the sanctuary? "They have taken my pew!" No new people? "The church is dying, and it's all *your* fault." These discontented folks keep us humble. While we need that sometimes, at other times, we need to ignore their grumbling (politely, of course) and rejoice instead.

When hearts are touched, when God is praised, when something really wonderful has happened—take the time to enjoy it. Revel in it. Call your friends and tell them all about it. Bore your spouse with all the details—again. It feels really good to do something well and to see a spark of life in a church you're growing to love.

Enjoy the times when you have worked hard and the labor pays off. You deserve a pat on the back for your part in the accomplishment. And then, praise the Lord for the success and give God the glory. Thank God for the ideas and the strength to pull everything together, for all the people who were involved, and for the hearts that were touched.

31

I told you so

I therefore, a prisoner in the Lord, beg you to lead a life worthy of the calling to which you have been called, with all humility and gentleness, with patience, bearing with one another in love, making every effort to maintain the unity of the Spirit in the bond of peace.

—Ephesians 4:1–3

"And so I decided that if he thought living with his dad was so great, then they both could just go there," exclaimed the exasperated mother. Her two teenage boys were difficult, and she had been through a hard year with them. The solution, she had decided, was to send them to live with her ex-husband, an alcoholic who had remarried after their divorce. While only one son wanted to go, they were both being shipped westward.

When I tried to ascertain whether the father was dry now, she said she wasn't sure. I wondered aloud if his new wife, just having had a baby, wanted to have the older kids there. "I don't know or care," she declared. "It's their father's problem, not mine. I've had them for ten years. It's his turn."

Concerned that the children might be headed into a situation where they weren't wanted, I asked how the father was preparing for their arrival. "Oh, I'll just call him when the plane takes off so he can't back out." Amazed at the mother's seeming lack of concern for her children's welfare, I tried to convince her to call and talk to him at least about this decision. She refused.

Not surprisingly, the summer was a disaster. The new wife was resentful. The father didn't know what to do with two teenagers and gave them free rein, with no curfews or rules. By the end of the summer, they had experimented with drugs and stayed out for days at a time. When their dad sent them home at the end of the summer, their mother had worse problems than she had had three months earlier.

I needed every bit of self-control I possessed not to shout, "I told you so, I told you so! Why didn't you listen to me? This is exactly what I told you might happen." Instead, I tried to help her focus on how to handle her current situation.

As pastors forced to stand by and watch people make self-destructive decisions, we get frustrated and even angry. Pray today for the people in your care who are making some seemingly unwise decisions. Pray that they would seek God's guidance and wisdom. Ask that God would grant you the patience you need to be with them, to advise them when they'll let you, and to help pick up the pieces when things fall apart.

32

Quenching your thirst

I pray that, according to the riches of his glory, he may grant that you may be strengthened in your inner being with power through his Spirit, and that Christ may dwell in your hearts through faith, as you are being rooted and grounded in love. I pray that you may have the power to comprehend, with all the saints, what is the breadth and length and height and depth, and to know the love of Christ that surpasses knowledge, so that you may be filled with all the fullness of God.

—EPHESIANS 3:16–19

WHEN I READ SOMEWHERE THAT LESS THAN HALF OF ALL PASTORS pray for thirty minutes a day, that didn't surprise me. What *did* shock me was that 10 percent of pastors spend more than an hour every day in prayer. I was stunned. I didn't do *anything* for more than an hour a day—except perhaps sermon preparation or maybe sleep. (Never at the same time, of course!)

My days are so fragmented and full of interruptions, I confessed to myself, *that if I had an entire hour, I doubt I would spend it praying.*

Life hadn't always been that way. In seminary, my prayer life had been so much better! We had daily chapel services and prayer partners and prayer before every class. I was immersed in a life of prayer. But in the pastorate, things had changed. The balance had subtly shifted.

Consequently, my walk with God was suffering. My time in the Word was limited to sermon and Bible study preparation. My prayers were quick and hurried, on-the-run obligations. I was less in tune with God's desire for my life and for the church. The time had come for a change.

A commitment to pray and absorb God's Word is not easy, but it makes all the difference in what kind of experience we have as pastors. Are you spending time with God every day? Have you set aside periods for study, prayer, and reflection? Ask God to show you any weaknesses in your spiritual walk, and seek the Holy Spirit's strength to make the necessary changes. ❧

33

The best gift

I thank my God every time I remember you, constantly praying with joy in every one of my prayers for all of you, because of your sharing in the gospel from the first day until now. I am confident of this, that the one who began a good work among you will bring it to completion by the day of Jesus Christ.

—PHILIPPIANS 1:3–6

ONE OF THE MOST SPECIAL GIFTS THAT MY MEMBERS HAVE GIVEN ME is letting me know that they pray for me. I appreciate knowing that they pray for my family and my ministry and for my own strength and encouragement. I am convinced those prayers are what get me through the hardest times. I covet their prayers. We all—clergy and laity alike—need to have people praying for us.

Once I understood that, I realized I was neglecting an important area of my ministry to my congregation. While I regularly prayed for those who were shut-in or ill or in mourning, I was not praying systematically for all of my members on a regular basis. And if I'm not praying for them, who is? Part of my responsibility as their pastor is to pray for them.

Now I go through the rolls regularly and pray for each member and each person who attends our church. Some pastors call and ask if the family has any needs, but I just pray. Pastors need to pray for our people—for their families, their jobs, their children, their friendships, and most of all, for their walks with the Lord. We must pray that they might seek to know God more thoroughly and walk with God more closely.

Begin praying for your members regularly. Go to the Lord on their behalf. This ministry of intercession will be a blessing to your members, even as their prayers are a blessing to you. ❧

34

Without need

Not that I am referring to being in need;
for I have learned to be content with whatever I have.
I know what it is to have little, and I know what it is
to have plenty. In any and all circumstances
I have learned the secret of being well-fed and of
going hungry, of having plenty and of being in need.
I can do all things through him who strengthens me.

—PHILIPPIANS 4:11–13

I DREAD THE ANNUAL TELEPHONE CALL FROM OUR ACCOUNTANT because she calls to tell us how much my spouse and I owe in taxes for the year. Because I am a self-employed pastor, we are responsible for paying the thousands and thousands of dollars annually to the IRS; no employer withholds the money each week on my behalf. Committed to keeping our daughter out of daycare, I am the primary wage earner in the family, allowing my spouse to be primary care giver. Our single income makes the end of each month a tight squeeze for us financially, and so not much is left-over at the end of the year to pay the taxes.

Sometimes, as I wrestle with our financial worries, I feel resentful. After all, I have a graduate degree and several years of experience, but we still live, in a lot of ways, hand to mouth. And keeping my focus on ministry is difficult when I worry about the medical bills that insurance doesn't pay. I get discouraged—and I'm not the only pastor to struggle with such feelings.

But the blessing my family has seen again and again over these early years of ministry is that we have never been in need. God has always provided for us. We have been given hand-me-down clothes, garden produce, leftovers from church dinners, and numerous other gifts that helped us stretch the paycheck. We have never gone hungry or without shelter or even adequate clothing. Our dream of keeping Kaylyn out of daycare has been realized, and every now and then, we are able to go on a vacation or do something special as a family.

Changing your perspective on what your needs truly are is a first step toward feeling less resentful about what you don't have. Is this aspect of pastoral ministry a struggle for you? Are you trusting God for your finances? Be thankful for the evidences of God's faithfulness in providing for you and your family. ❧

35

Wise counsel

Get wisdom; get insight: do not forget, nor turn away
from the words of my mouth.
Do not forsake her, and she will keep you;
love her, and she will guard you.
The beginning of wisdom is this: Get wisdom,
and whatever else you do, get insight.

—PROVERBS 4:5–7

"OK, BILL, I HAVE MY FIRST ANNUAL PASTORAL EVALUATION FORM, and I need to evaluate my own job performance," I explained to my friend and mentor.

"Those are always fun. How is it going?" he asked.

"Fine, I think. I just have one question."

"What is it?"

"Do you think it's OK to give myself a ninety-eight for the score?"

"That depends. Ninety-eight out of how many?"

"One hundred."

I moved the phone away from my ear as he laughed heartily. "Going for the modest approach, I see. I'm not sure Jesus would have given *himself* a ninety-eight. I would go back to the drawing board."

"All right, all right." I admitted that there were probably one or two more things that I needed to work on in the upcoming year. When I submitted the revised form, nobody on my evaluation committee laughed. Bill, as it turned out, had been right. Better that he laugh than my committee!

One of the blessings God has given me is a mentor willing to listen, offer suggestions, and brainstorm with me. Sometimes mentors can be difficult to find, but all pastors need that kind of support and accountability. A mentor's counsel can make the first few years of pastoring go a little more smoothly than they would have otherwise. I know I am grateful for what my mentor offers.

If you don't have a mentoring relationship but would like one, pray that God would provide the right person. If you do have such an adviser, thank God for the counsel he or she offers your ministry. ❧

36

Heart on your sleeve

Let the word of Christ dwell in you richly; teach and admonish one another in all wisdom; and with gratitude in your hearts sing psalms, hymns, and spiritual songs to God. And whatever you do, in word or deed, do everything in the name of the Lord Jesus, giving thanks to God the Father through him.

—COLOSSIANS 3:16–17

"NICE SERMON, AS ALWAYS, PASTOR," THEY SAID AS THEY SMILED, shook my hand, and walked out of the sanctuary. *Nice sermon?* I wanted to ask. *Nice sermon? I agonized over that sermon for days! All you can say is that it was nice? What about thought-provoking or poignant or life-changing?* I shook my head in frustration and went home, where my family was waiting.

"Nice sermon, dear," said my husband as I entered the kitchen. I narrowly avoided hitting him with a dish towel. Then, later in the week, I received a call from a church member who wanted me to know that the sermon had touched her and helped her make some critical life-decisions.

For pastors, preaching every week is like wearing our heart on our sleeve. We want so much to reach our people in a meaningful way. And so we share some of our life-story, how this particular Scripture has influenced us and how our walk with God has been affected. Unfortunately, sometimes, that intensely personal sermon falls flat, and our folks just don't seem to respond.

But be encouraged! There are also other times—times when your people are in your hand and with you. You can see it in their faces. Those are the worship experiences when God so directs your sermons so that they intimately tie into the hearts of your people—when lives are changed. On those Sundays, you can almost feel a sense of "Aaahhh!" resonating through the sanctuary.

Pray that the Lord would be present with you as you prepare your sermons. Ask that the Spirit would put the needs of your members to the forefront of your mind so that those concerns guide your sermons and so that your messages will better minister to God's people. ❧

37

Jesus who?

All over the world this gospel
is bearing fruit and growing,
just as it has been doing among you.
—COLOSSIANS 1:6, *PARAPHRASED*

"I DON'T UNDERSTAND, TEACHER. WHY DID THEY KILL HIM? AND how did this guy Jesus know God, anyway?" Used to teaching children raised in the church, I was surprised that this little girl did not know the story of Jesus. As the new Sunday school teacher for the primary class, I looked down, wondering if perhaps she was joking. She wasn't. Her dark eyes looked up at me, innocent and curious. She simply didn't know who Jesus was, why he had come, and what meaning that held for her.

Taken aback for a minute or so, I realized that I don't encounter many people who have never heard about Jesus. Church members have heard the gospel over and over again. Even people outside the church have already heard the story, although they have not yet chosen to respond to the Good News by making a personal commitment to Christ. What a responsibility and honor to be able to introduce someone to Jesus for the very first time! *That* is why I accepted God's call to ministry in the first place.

And yet, pastors have so many other responsibilities, sometimes we struggle to maintain that initial level of passion and excitement we have for sharing our faith. We get caught up in doctrinal discussions and the everyday concerns involved in keeping a church afloat. But every once in a while, God will provide a nudge and gently remind us about the purpose of our calling.

Pray that the Lord will open the door this week for you to share the story of Christ with someone new. Ask God to direct your conversations, and then follow the Spirit's leading. ❧

38

Walking in the gray area

Be strong and courageous; do not be frightened or dismayed, for the Lord your God is with you wherever you go.

—Joshua 1:9

As I was enjoying the morning paper, a member of the congregation telephoned to tell me how much she had appreciated my sermon the day before. It had been life-changing, she said, and made the Scripture come alive like never before.

The phone rang again a few minutes later. Still basking in the warm compliments, I was unprepared for what came next.

"You are absolutely the worst pastor I have ever heard of," screeched the angry woman. "You had no right to do what you did. It was inexcusable." With that as the starting point, the conversation went downhill from there. She was furious over a decision I had a made, and she let me have it with both barrels. I could understand her point; it was valid. The decision had been a judgment call that could have gone either way. And yet, I did have a good reason for doing what I had done. (The only slightly amusing aspect of the situation was that this irate member wanted to transfer her membership from our church, a place where she hadn't darkened the threshold in twenty years.

At least, I couldn't help thinking to myself, *we won't have to pay our dues on her membership to the denomination anymore.*)

When issues are not clear-cut and as pastors we have to make decisions that have an impact on others, the consequences can be tough. This is especially true when we are fairly sure we have made the right decision—but not completely. It can be agonizing when people say we have made a bad decision and respond in anger. We rehash every nuance of the decision, lose sleep over the consequent confrontation, and generally blow the entire situation way out of proportion. When you find yourself in such a circumstance, the best you can do is give the matter over to God, seek wise counsel, and pray for a healing in the broken relationship. ❧

39

Hand-me-down love

For every wild animal of the forest is mine,
the cattle on a thousand hills.

—Psalm 50:10

I am reminded of the pastors of old who used to get paid in chickens. So far this week I have received a hideous, brown, polyester, hand-me-down dress, a dozen eggs, a few previously read magazines (which I enjoy), and an invitation out to dinner for our family. At Christmas, we are given candy, bread, cookies, and an assortment of gifts, from books to knick-knacks. In the summer, anonymous bags of tomatoes, zucchini, summer squash, zucchini, cucumbers, and zucchini are left on the back porch. (Did I mention zucchini?) Once, when a family member died and I had to fly home suddenly, an envelope with money was quietly given.

The generosity of the people can feel overwhelming sometimes. While I have to admit, I have passed on a few items to the Goodwill store, I appreciate the thought behind each gift. Every time I reach for the eggs or make another loaf of zucchini bread, I know that we are loved, both by God and God's people in this place.

As pastors, accepting gifts graciously may mean letting go of our pride, but it also means receiving more blessings than we can count. We need to allow members to give to us and to accept those gifts graciously. Refusing to accept such gifts robs the giver of a blessing.

Think of some of the ways that your people show their care and concern for you and your family. Thank God now for the generosity of your church family. Let the Lord know how much you appreciate how the Spirit uses your members to show God's love and abundance. ❧

40

Home away from home

What God has planned
for the people who love him
is more than eyes have seen
or ears have heard.
It has never even entered our minds!

—1 CORINTHIANS 2:9, CEV

EVERY SPRING, MIDDLE C ON THE PIANO IN THE SANCTUARY GETS horribly out of tune. The handle on the toilet in the men's restroom must be jiggled just right, or else the water runs all week. The doors on the west side of the church never lock on the first try; they require a kick, a twist, and a silent threat to replace the lock before they cooperate. And the ushers always show new visitors just where to sit—fifth pew from the back, organ side—so that none of the regulars get mad at having their seat taken.

Pastors need a little time to feel at home in a new place. This place does now for me, but I've been here for two years. I don't miss the last church quite as much, but I have my days. Even though I moved just a few hundred miles away, the distance feels like a million. With every Sunday that passes, however, I let go of a little more homesickness. Feeling as though I belong in a strange new world like this isn't easy, but I'm getting more comfortable. The decision to stop pining for home was a hard one to make, but I knew the homesickness was keeping me from fully acclimating to life in a new church.

And so, I have grown to love the feel of the sanctuary, dark and quiet. Under my hands, I feel where the pulpit has been worn smooth by decades of preaching. I like to watch the morning sun sparkle through the cool, blue stones of the stained-glass cross. When the phone rings at 8:30 A.M., I smile because I know who is calling. At last, I feel like I belong.

The gift of having a new church come to feel like home is a precious one for us as pastors. Embrace it. Be thankful for where God has placed you. Tell the Lord about the things you love there. Ask God to open your eyes to see more of the beauty yet to be discovered. ❧

41

A few weeds and a lot of patience

Since God chose you to be the holy people whom he loves, you must clothe yourselves with tenderhearted mercy, kindness, humility, gentleness, and patience. You must make allowance for each other's faults and forgive the person who offends you. Remember, the Lord forgave you, so you must forgive others. And the most important piece of clothing you must wear is love. Love is what binds us all together in perfect harmony.

—COLOSSIANS 3:12–14, NLT

WE HAD ONLY BEEN IN THE PARSONAGE A FEW DAYS WHEN A TEARFUL elderly woman came knocking on the front door. Immediately concerned and wondering what disaster could have befallen her, I ushered her into the living room where I had been sitting with my husband. As she sat down, she tried to catch her breath, but the tears started to flow freely again. She reached across the couch and into the laundry basket that sat on the floor, pulling out a pair of my toddler's training pants which were (thankfully) newly washed. With a loud honk, she blew her nose while I silently willed my husband not to laugh.

As the woman's story unfolded, we discovered the source of her grief. Someone had dug up her flower patch behind the church. Apparently, a well-meaning trustee had been doing yard work and spotted a few too many of what he considered weeds. A few tugs later and a dozen or so flowers were gone. The result wasn't pretty. And this woman was incredibly upset. For weeks, every time the subject came up, she burst into tears.

I struggled to be patient with her after the first few days. I am able to brush off most minor problems, and I can be judgmental when others don't react the same way that I do. My tendency was to say, "Look, they were just flowers. You can plant new ones. This is not a big deal!" I had enough self-control to refrain—and that was a good thing.

As pastors, we need to allow folks to express hurt over even small things. Granted, sometimes the hurt and accompanying feelings of anger or resentment may drag on for such a time that pastoral intervention becomes necessary to help repair relationships. I have found, however, that for the most part, a little patience will go a long way.

Do you struggle with impatience when your members are upset over seemingly minor issues? Ask God to help you be more sensitive to your members and have the compassion and strength to intervene when necessary. ❧

42

Family circus

If you put these instructions before the brothers and sisters, you will be a good servant of Christ Jesus, nourished on the words of the faith and of the sound teaching that you have followed.

—1 TIMOTHY 4:6

THE GREAT-GRANDFATHER LAY BACK IN HIS HOSPITAL BED AND TRIED to explain to his son that he felt abandoned and betrayed by his family's lack of concern and attention. My heart went out to the old man because I sensed just how difficult this must have been for him to finally admit. I glanced at the son, hoping he would be sensitive to his father's obvious pain. I was disappointed.

Instead, my mouth dropped open as the younger man began singing a rather poor rendition of an old Harry Chapin tune, "Cat's in the Cradle." The lyrics are poignant and tell the story about a father who is too busy working to be a good father and about how, years later, the son is too wrapped up in his own life to be a good son. *Perhaps the scenario is true in this family as well,* I acknowledged, *but this sure isn't a thoughtful way to respond to a sick man's pain.* I felt as though I were in a bad play as I watched sadness and hopelessness wash over the old man like a wave. The son, who was focused on justifying his decisions, was oblivious to his dad's pain.

I am continually amazed at the ways families treat each other. I am surprised by the lack of loyalty, trust, and honor in marriages and between generations. Weddings can be the worst occasions for revealing such brokenness of relationship. Not a wedding etiquette book out there can adequately prepare a minister for the tangle of relational nightmares that will appear in a single wedding party. Recently I had to get a bridegroom to draw a diagram of his wedding party because I just couldn't get a handle on who couldn't be beside whom and why—because this one was divorced from that one and these two weren't speaking to those three.

A steady diet of such heartbreak isn't easy for pastors to stomach. We hate to watch people hurt one another, especially within their own families. Think about the families in pain in your church. In what ways can you better minister to them?

43

Tag-along preachers

They devoted themselves to the apostles' teaching and fellowship, to the breaking of bread and the prayers. . . . All who believed were together and held all things in common.

—ACTS 2:42,44

THE COOL, CRISP BREEZE SWEPT ACROSS THE FIELD, REMINDING US that winter was anxious to arrive. On the chilly Sunday afternoon, my family and I were camped out on the sidelines with another family from the church, watching their son play in a Pee-Wee football game. Other than asking how many home runs the team had, I didn't seem to reveal too much of my ignorance about the game. Although my attention wandered often, I yelled and cheered when his family did. We had a good time, all wrapped in warm sweaters and good friendships. I remember the laughter, but not the score.

Pastors belong in the pulpit and by hospital beds and visiting shut-ins. At least, that's what I used to think. However, while I don't neglect those things, I also spend a lot of time watching basketball games and going out to eat and enjoying other activities that, at least at first glance, have nothing to do with ministry. When I'm invited, I go. Or when I know about a special event involving one of my parishioners, I get tickets. When the occasion matters to my folks, I want to be there.

Building relationships takes *time.* I admit that the task would be more convenient if the goal were more easily attained. But our folks only get to know us, trust us, and believe what we say in the pulpit or counseling session if they spend time with us beyond an hour of corporate worship once a week. As pastors, we need to be constantly on the lookout for ways to build stronger relationships with our people.

Examine the ways you have gotten to know your members. How can you build stronger relationships with them? Ask God for insight. ❧

44

To the rescue

And God is able to provide you with every blessing in abundance, so that by always having enough of everything, you may share abundantly in every good work.

—2 CORINTHIANS 9:8

"DID YOU KNOW THAT THEY TAKE AWAY YOUR SHOE LACES WHEN YOU come in here?"

I raised my eyebrows slightly. "Nope . . . didn't know that. Glad I wore my loafers in here then."

Glancing around the sparsely furnished room, I was desperate for something to say. Turning away from the bar-covered windows, I finally took a closer look at Kristen. Pale and dark eyed, she leaned back against the headboard with her knees pulled up to her chin. Her long, dark hair hung lankly over her shoulders, her thin wrists securely bandaged, covering the self-inflicted wounds of the night before.

"How are things today?" The question seemed inadequate, but I just didn't know what else to say. What I wanted to say, I couldn't: *Why? Why couldn't you call me? Why this?* I wondered if a better pastor would have been more helpful, if someone else would have seen the signs.

Searching for the right words, I found none. Instead I sat on the bed beside her and looked out the window with her. The silence was peaceful, even as we were aware of loud noises down the hall. We watched the sun turn into a brilliant gold as it dipped low in the horizon. It seemed to promise a better tomorrow.

Feeling comfortable with silence isn't always easy. I always want to fix everyone's problems, to make everything all right. But, sometimes the most pastoral thing to do is just sit and be with someone, *without* having all the right answers. Be sensitive and know that your presence alone can be a word of hope. Ask God to give you a spirit that discerns the time to speak and the time to be silent. ❧

45

Staying the course

I rejoice at your word
like one who finds great spoil. . . .
Great peace have those who love your law;
nothing can make them stumble.
I hope for your salvation, O LORD,
and I fulfill your commandments.
My soul keeps your decrees;
I love them exceedingly.

—PSALM 119:162,165–167

I WANTED TO QUIT. MENTALLY, I BEGAN PACKING MY BAGS. IT HAD become painfully obvious that I just wasn't cut out for the ministry. *I wasn't just reacting to one thing,* I assured myself, *but to a hundred different things.* I had done everything my leadership books had told me to do, and the promised results weren't there. Our numbers were only slightly higher than they had been when I arrived two years earlier, and the church's checking account was dwindling fast.

Some members were beginning to prophesy doom. Could I really wipe out with one fell swoop a church that had withstood one-hundred-fifty years of ministry? What to do? I was discouraged, wondering if the church might be better if I just left. After all, it didn't seem as if the situation could get much worse.

After I had moped around the house for a few days, I chastised myself for neglecting the most minimal of my pastoral duties and sped to the hospital to see a church member or two. My final visit was with Ray, an old man whose wife had just been put in a nursing home with Alzheimer's. Now the disease seemed to be claiming him as well. I sat and held Ray's hand, listening as he recounted everything he had lost in the last year—his wife, his home, his driving privileges, and now his mind. "It seems like more than a body could take," he whispered.

I pulled out my Bible and opened it up to some of my favorite passages. "This is what I read when I feel discouraged, Ray," I answered. "Let's hear God's word to you right now." And as the Word ministered to Ray's heart, tears began to fall silently down his cheeks. He squeezed my hand, then patted it. "Don't stop," he urged. "I need more of that."

Me too, Ray. Me too. All pastors experience some feelings of discouragement in ministry, no matter how diligent and generally effective we are. When those feelings come, go to God in prayer and search the Scriptures to hear God's word to you.

46

Diversionary tactics

Come to me, all you that are weary and are
carrying heavy burdens, and I will give you rest.
Take my yoke upon you, and learn from me;
for I am gentle and humble in heart,
and you will find rest for your souls.

—Matthew 11:28–29

"Oh, when the saints—" I frowned and started over. "Oh, when the saints come marching in—" I winced as I struck the wrong note (again). But with another hour of practice, I ended up with a somewhat passable rendition. However, my main criteria in pursuing perfection with practice has been that someone walking by would at least hear some resemblance to a familiar tune. On that afternoon, my playing wasn't pretty, but it sure was progress. In another few weeks, I would be ready to perform for my gathered clan of child, husband, and cats.

Within a few months of beginning full-time ministry, I realized I needed a distraction. My entire life was consumed by either my job or my family. And while I love both, I found it was becoming increasingly difficult for me to relax and wind down at the end of a difficult day. Some pastors play golf; others knit or read. I wanted to learn something new—and I didn't even know how to read music.

Learning to play an instrument has been worth every penny and every moment spent. I have measurable goals, and to my delight, I soon perceive my own progress, something that is not always true in the ministry. But what I love most about my new hobby is that I can escape from my office for half an hour in the middle of my day and lose myself in the music. Then, I can go back to office, refreshed and renewed and ready to deal with whatever the rest of the day brings. That piano bench helps keep my life balanced.

Pastors need that kind of balance. We need to indulge interests utterly apart from our ministries and other obligations. Look at how your life is divided. Have you allowed yourself the time and resources for what you enjoy? Praise God for the activities and relationships that keep you healthy, and be sure to foster those sources of refreshment and joy.

47

Hasty decisions

For we do not have a high priest who is unable to sympathize with our weaknesses, but we have one who in every respect has been tested as we are, yet without sin. Let us therefore approach the throne of grace with boldness, so that we may receive mercy and find grace to help in time of need.

—HEBREWS 4:15–16

WAITING FOR THE BRIDE TO COME UP THE AISLE, I GLANCED AROUND the sanctuary decorated with dozens of red roses. The bride's attendants wore long red evening gowns, and the groomsmen were in black tuxedos. As the bride came down the aisle, the few family and friends who were gathered admired her elegant white wedding dress, although they were surprised at the extravagance in what was a second wedding. I smiled at the congregation but tried to avoid looking into the bride's father's eyes. I knew what I would see.

Agreeing to officiate at this wedding had been a mistake. I had known it almost immediately after I acquiesced. And yet, I had given my word and was too stubborn to recant. Now I was left with the consequences. Watching heartbroken parents witness a wedding that shouldn't have taken place, I needed every ounce of strength I had to complete the service and not just walk away in the middle of the ceremony.

As I left the sanctuary at the end of the service, I was embarrassed for having taken the easy way out, for not doing the honorable thing and doing what I believed was right. Taking off my robe, I dropped my wedding manual on my chair and walked out of the church, still avoiding the eyes of the bride's father.

Furious with myself, I felt guilty for months. My regrets came too late; I couldn't go back and make the right decision. I could only try not to make the wrong decision twice. At some point in our ministries, all pastors make mistakes, and then we are faced with a choice. What do we do with the regrets and the guilt? Do we let them consume us, or do we acknowledge them and accept a lesson learned the hard way?

Think about the mistakes you may have made already in your ministry. Have you forgiven yourself for them? Ask God to help you learn from your mistakes, and then let go of them. ❧

48

Rest for the weary

For thus said the Lord God, the Holy One of Israel:
In returning and rest you shall be saved;
in quietness and in trust shall be your strength.

—Isaiah 30:15

I confess. On Sunday afternoons, I like to sneak back over to church. Usually barefoot and in my comfortable clothes, I spend a few hours there. I like to file away my sermon and straighten my desk for the next workday. Everything should look neat and ready for Tuesday morning. And sometimes on Mondays, my day off, I come in, too. But I don't stay long—just long enough to dash off a quick letter and make a telephone call or two.

My sermon about the Sabbath is very good. In fact, it is one of my best. The only problem is that I don't pay attention to its message myself. Not a word of it. Rationalizing to myself, I say that it is hardly reasonable for pastors to take two whole days off a week. *If I get a few free hours here and there,* I reason, *it counts the same.* However, a few scattered hours of leisure do not a sabbath rest make, and I know it.

I have come to realize that I *do* need two days off in a week. In my first year of ministry, I went for five consecutive months without any sort of vacation other than my sporadic day off. That wasn't a good plan. I was irritable and less patient than usual, and I found myself creating large issues out of relatively minor ones. Even though I was working without rest, my sermons were not as well prepared and my illustrations were weak.

God's expectations about work and rest are clear—and pastors are not exempt from the larger human race in this matter. When we work, we are to be faithful and diligent. But we are to be intentional about creating opportunities to honor the Sabbath as well—not only by setting aside the Sabbath day but also by taking a sabbath rest in the midst of our busy week. We can't afford not to.

Consider *your* faithfulness to the divine mandate of a Sabbath. What changes do you need to make in your lifestyle and schedule to make time and space for a sabbath rest? Pray that you would be disciplined and humble enough to find your strength in quietness and trust.

49

Me, a servant?

Let the same mind be in you that was in Christ Jesus,
who, though he was in the form of God,
did not regard equality with God
as something to be exploited,
but emptied himself,
taking the form of a slave,
being born in human likeness.
And being found in human form,
he humbled himself
and became obedient to the point of death—
even death on a cross.

—PHILIPPIANS 2:5–8

"I DON'T CARE WHAT YOU SAY. I AM NOT GOING TO A NURSING home!" announced Martha loudly. "My friends at church can help me just fine."

I couldn't reason with her, couldn't get her to understand that no matter how many people tried to help her, our efforts just weren't enough. Alone at age eighty-eight, Martha needed more assistance than we could provide. The handful of helpers were simply overwhelmed. I myself was tempted to leave my phone off the hook so I wouldn't get called in the middle of the night to go help her. Even considering it made me feel guilty. When

Martha was admitted to the local hospital the day after our discussion, the burden of her care was lifted from the church members, at least temporarily.

Then, a week or so later, a note came from Martha's niece, one of her few relatives. Because her own health was poor, the seventy-year-old niece could do little for her aunt. "I wanted to thank you," she wrote. "You and the church family take real good care of Aunt Martha. I don't go to church much, and I don't know a lot about God," she continued. "But when she tells me everything you all do for her, it sounds like you're just like Jesus. I wish I could be like that."

Hot tears streamed down my cheeks as I read and reread that letter. I knew that I had been no more like Jesus to Martha than the man in the moon was. I had lost my attitude of servitude. In spite of that, somebody had seen Jesus in me. That's what I want to be about as a pastor.

Often as pastors, we may be torn between the very real needs of our individual members and the limited resources of the church congregation. In doing what we can with the resources we have, we may struggle against a spirit of frustration or defensiveness and our service may become anything but Christlike. That God is still able to reveal Jesus through such imperfect ministry is a miracle not to be exploited.

In what areas of your ministry do you lack a servant attitude? Let your prayer today be that people would see Jesus in you.

Sacrificial lambs

We do not live to ourselves, and we do not die to ourselves.
If we live, we live to the Lord, and if we die, we die to the Lord;
so then, whether we live or whether we die, we are the Lord's.

—ROMANS 14:7–8

"I JUST LOVE THAT JACKET YOU HAVE ON," SAID THE FLIGHT ATTENDANT to the gentleman behind me in line. "Where do I get a jacket like that?" I turned for a quick look and saw that the man had an obviously expensive wool jacket with the emblem of a famous sports network emblazoned on the front.

"This jacket is very expensive," explained the man quietly. "To be allowed to wear a jacket like this, I have to give up my children's birthday parties and my wedding anniversaries and this week, my daughter's first ballet recital. That's how you get to wear a jacket like this. Does it still interest you?"

Embarrassed, the flight attendant looked down and shook his head. He decided it was time to help another passenger. As I sat down, I looked at the man in the jacket. He had the saddest eyes. Since then, I have often thought about that man and the sacrifices he and his family were making. In a sense, they were empty sacrifices. He was giving up tremendous amounts of time with his family so that he could adequately provide for them, but he had lost a great deal in the process.

Pastors are often guilty of the same thing, albeit not often for financial rewards. We have so much work to do building up the Kingdom and taking care of our members that sometimes, we leave our families in the dust. Unless we specifically consider our families' needs and how they are being met, pastors also run the risk of letting our families suffer.

How much time are you spending with your family? Are the hours you allot to them enough? Thank God today for the blessing of your family. ❧

Comfort zone

But each of us was given grace according to the measure of Christ's gift. . . . The gifts he gave were that some should be apostles, some prophets, some evangelists, some pastors and teachers, to equip the saints for the work of ministry, . . .

—EPHESIANS 4:7,11–12

AS THE PERSON DRAMATIZING JESUS WALKED OFF THE STAGE AND between the pews, a holy hush came upon the sanctuary. It was the perfect ending to the Easter service. The play had been a good one, and the actors had done well. I was so proud of them. What I had enjoyed the most about the play was seeing the involvement of a few members who tended to do not much more than attend Sunday morning worship.

Helping people to stretch and move beyond their comfort level is an enjoyable reward of being in the ministry. The church can be a safe, supportive environment in which to try something new, whether that something is a new skill, such as acting or cooking, or just taking new risks in building new relationships. For many people, the idea of sitting in a Sunday school class and opening up to a entire group of people is terrifying. As pastors, we need to strike a balance between finding ways for people to use their gifts and helping them to be open to new experiences.

The same holds true for pastors. We shouldn't ask anyone to do something that we are unwilling to do ourselves. After struggling to recruit enough children's Sunday school teachers, I realized that in all my years in the church, I had never taught a single children's class. I do now. The experience is a good stretch for me and a good model for my people. They see that I am willing to do something that is not within my comfort zone. They see that I am willing to trust God for the results and that God is ever faithful.

Seek to be sensitive to people in your congregation who may need an extra effort to feel included. As new opportunities to minister arise, don't just look to the same half-dozen people who are already doing everything. Consider, too: are you, yourself, open to being used in ministry in a different way? ❧

52

Nickels and noses

. . . I say to everyone among you not to think of yourself more highly than you ought to think, but to think with sober judgment, each according to the measure of faith that God has assigned.

—Romans 12:3

MOST PASTORS REPORT THEIR WORSHIP ATTENDANCE FIGURES ONLY IN round numbers. In fact, every pastor I have ever heard comment on the attendance has said something to the effect of, "We had 120 last week" or "This Sunday we had 220 people." While those figures may be accurate, I suspect that the pastors are rounding to the next figure—and that they always round up, not down. Why would I assume this? Because I have caught myself doing the same thing a time or two. If eighty-one people were in attendance, surely that's close enough to count as ninety, right?

The temptation to play the numbers game is a strong one for pastors. We want so much to be successful at this calling. After all, this is what we have been trained to do. We are fresh out of seminary and supposedly filled with new ideas and dreams. If we can't pastor, then who can? And the easiest way to judge how well we are doing seems to be by counting nickels and noses. Unfortunately, those numbers rarely reveal the whole story.

Numbers don't reflect the progress you saw a young couple make in their premarital counseling sessions. Or the lives that were changed among the mouths that were fed through the new food pantry. The numbers don't show how many relationships were forged over a cup of coffee and a visit on a quiet afternoon or the impact of the quiet prayers spoken beside the bedside of an old, tired, and confused man.

Ask the Lord to help you see where progress is being made in your service and how God's name is being glorified in the Spirit's ministry through you. ❧

53

A job well done

Do your best to present yourself to God
as one approved by him, a worker who has no need to be
ashamed, rightly explaining the word of truth.

—2 Timothy 2:15

We shuffled through our papers again, not wanting to see what we thought we had seen—right there in black and white. Within a five mile radius of our small church in the cornfields, the biggest need of our community was adequate food. Families all around us were going to bed hungry at night because they didn't have the resources to purchase what they needed. It was a sobering thought.

And as the group examined dozens of other pieces of data about the community, we were drawn back again and again to the problem of hunger. The image of children suffering around us was horrifying. Finally, one member cleared his throat and said, "The purpose of this study was to look at what we could do to attract new members. I don't care about that anymore. We can't just sit here and ignore this." Within a few weeks, a plan was born. Within a few months, a food pantry was opened. Forty-five people were served in the first four weeks of its existence, four hundred in the first three months.

I was so proud of my church. They had seen a problem and were willing to roll up their sleeves and do what it took to meet the needs of those around them. Pastors ought to rejoice in the times when our congregations do *right.* They deserve recognition and praise for a job well done.

Thank the Lord today for members willing to work hard for the Kingdom. Pray for them and their families, that they would not grow discouraged. Find ways to support and encourage them in *their* ministries. ❧

54

Whoa, Nelly!

I wait for the LORD, my soul waits,
and in his word I hope;
my soul waits for the Lord
more than those who watch for the morning,
more than those who watch for the morning.

—PSALM 130:5–6

"IF I WERE YOU, ANGIE, I WOULD JUST STEP BACK AND WAIT A FEW weeks to see what happens with this project before jumping into another. Of course, you don't have to take my advice. . . ." I grimaced as I listened to what I didn't want to hear, although I knew my adviser was probably right.

Every few weeks of my ministry, I need to remind myself to put on the brakes and step back. I tend to act first and think later. Although my first inclination when I arrived at my new church was to jump in and fix the first few dozen problems I identified, I did know enough to stop, wait, and focus on building relationships first.

But once the first year was over, I found myself making grand plans first and only considering the response of my people after 99 percent of the work was already done. Too often, I didn't even pray first and seek what God wanted. I assumed that if I had the idea, God must have given it to me so I could implement it right away. This wasn't the most efficient way to work because I spent so much time explaining myself to other people and defending my plan.

So many pastors cut their own ministries short because they aren't willing to wait to get to know the people first and see what needs to happen second. Instead, we would be so much more effective if we went to one or two people that we know well and trust, who seem to have their fingers on the pulse of the congregation, and sounded them out first.

Do you have someone who will advise you honestly about the wisdom and timing of your ideas? If so, then be thankful. Such an adviser is a priceless gift to an overzealous pastor! Seek the timing of the Lord when you devise grand schemes and brilliant ideas. God knows your church and your ministry intimately. Wait for the Spirit's leading and seek God's approval.

Thick-skinned

But he said to me, "My grace is sufficient for you,
for power is made perfect in weakness."
So, I will boast all the more gladly of my weaknesses,
so that the power of Christ may dwell in me. Therefore,
I am content with weaknesses, insults, hardships,
persecutions, and calamities for the sake of Christ;
for whenever I am weak, then I am strong.

—2 CORINTHIANS 12:9–10

"WELL, I'D SAY THAT THE DELIVERY AND THE CONTENT OF YOUR sermons have improved considerably within the last year." My heart stuck in my throat as I digested this piece of information as a part of my annual review. I had known that areas of improvement would be suggested, but the comment had caught me off guard. Had I been a horrible preacher a year ago? My delivery *and* the content. Not just one, but two harsh blows. My ego was crushed. My sermons were the one thing I thought I did well. Virtually ignoring the rest of the evaluation process, which would have been edifying, I fixated on those few comments. They whirled around in my head for weeks.

Because so much of what we do as pastors is tied intimately to who we are, criticism can be difficult to take. When the tasks we perform are critically evaluated, we may struggle to separate a critique of our performance from criticism of ourselves as people. Even constructive criticism can feel like a personal attack. Because of our own insecurities, we can't hear what is really being said. Our ministries don't feel like just a job. We are pastors twenty-four hours a day, seven days a week. Our ministries are who we are. But if our lives are too constricted, if *all* we are is a pastor, then criticism will become difficult to receive.

God has been at work stretching my life with the addition of some new hobbies and friends and interests. Consequently, my sense of perspective has broadened considerably. Yes, I still fall short in my ministry, but because my pastorate is just a portion of who I am, those areas of concern no longer define me.

Can you separate who you are from your ministry? Are you able to step back and be evaluated without feeling personally attacked? A good mentor can be helpful here. Give your ministry to God today. ❧

Blinded by the spotlight

. . . And all of you must clothe yourselves with humility in your dealings with one another, for
"God opposes the proud,
but gives grace to the humble."

—1 PETER 5:5

THREE NEWSPAPERS, FOUR TELEVISION STATIONS. THE PRESS RELEASES announcing a special event taking place in our small church were faxed into news offices. The highlight of the special service was to be a message brought by the local mayor, whose presence was an honor for the church. Then, twenty-four hours before the event was to take place, the mayor was indicted on charges of election fraud, bribery, and theft. The news created a media circus, and it was too late for our church to back out of the spotlight.

And yet, in the back of my mind, I thought quietly that maybe the situation was to our advantage after all. Certainly the media would come out now to catch a glimpse of the embattled mayor in perilous times. This would be our chance to shine. Finally, our church would get some attention! The day the news broke, I patted myself on the back a number of times for the perfect timing, while throwing up a half-hearted prayer for the mayor.

Not until the morning of the event did it dawn on me: I hadn't once prayed about the service. I had given no thought to how God would be glorified in the current situation. I suppose that I assumed that God would just naturally tag along with whatever I had planned. My spirit was contrite. I had planned this with only one thought—getting attention for the church and, ultimately, me. I was embarrassed by my motives and confessed them to God. The lesson was a painful one for me. Nevertheless, in the end, the Lord was lifted up in that service and the focus remained on God.

Pride is a difficult thorn for pastors. We want to do well and to have our people and our community think highly of us, and yet, our ultimate goal is to give glory to God. Examine your motives carefully. Seek God's help to expose prideful tendencies and to submit them to the Lord. ☙

Life in a fish bowl

You are the light of the world. A city built on a hill cannot be hid. No one after lighting a lamp puts it under the bushel basket, but on the lampstand, and it gives light to all in the house. In the same way, let your light shine before others, so that they may see your good works and give glory to your Father in heaven.

—MATTHEW 5:14–16

MONTHLY CHURCH DINNERS ARE A GOOD THING. THEY RAISE MONEY for mission projects, build a spirit of community, and provide a good opportunity for people of all generations to work together. Yet, they seem to crop up with alarming frequency. Every time I turn around, I'm supposed to be there—and not just attending but actually doing something to help out. The dinners can absorb most of one Saturday a month, ten months a year. I have come to see them as something of a necessary evil.

The problem is magnified because I live right next door to the church. If I just don't want to work that day, I am prisoner in my own house—especially in the summer. I furtively close the blinds over open windows, quiet my child, and hope no one calls to borrow something, because if they do, they will know I am home and not helping with the event. Sometimes living so close to the church isn't all it's cracked up to be.

Some pastors are criticized for how they trim the hedges, what they wear when they mow the lawn, and even how their children play in the yard. Imagine what members must think of a pastoral parent whose child is going through the terrible-twos (and threes)! Pastors can't hide much when we live ten yards from the church.

But today, make a decision to celebrate that. Rejoicing is much easier than resenting something that won't change. Ask God to help you rejoice that it's a short walk to the office, that you are closely entwined in the fabric of your church, and that sometimes, open windows keep you humble. ❧

Thy presence known

For it is the God who said, "Let light shine out of darkness," who has shone in our hearts to give the light of the knowledge of the glory of God in the face of Jesus Christ.

—2 CORINTHIANS 4:6

I CAN'T COUNT HOW MANY PASTORAL CALLS I HAVE MADE TO JAIL cells, hospital rooms, and nursing homes in my ministry. One would think I would be an expert by now. Sadly, that is not the case. Sometimes the visits go well; other times I don't have any idea what to say. I am ashamed to confess I have resorted to talking about the weather more than once. Nothing is worse than sitting by a hospital bed, saying, "Well, it sure is a rainy day today."

This time was different. I sat by the hospital bed and asked how her spirits were holding up. They were down, she admitted. But then she added, "On my way to the hospital this morning, I looked out and saw a cardinal. I listened as it sang so beautifully." Tears welled up in her eyes as she softly spoke, "And then God reminded me of the old song, 'His Eye Is on the Sparrow.' It was such a comfort to me—even though the doctors don't know what's wrong with me," she gestured toward the monitors and intravenous accouterments that surrounded her. "I know that God is watching over me, and that makes it easier."

I held her hand, and we prayed together, "Thank you, God, for making your presence known. . . ."

Go into pastoral calls seeking the heavenly Father's words for his children. Be reminded that you bring comfort and hope as you minister to the sick and broken. Spend time praying before you enter their rooms, and don't neglect the opportunity to pray with *them* before you leave. ❧

Grace and eviction notices

If there is among you anyone in need, a member of your community in any of your towns within the land that the LORD your God is giving you, do not be hard-hearted or tight-fisted toward your needy neighbor. You should rather open your hand, willingly lending enough to meet the need, whatever it may be.

—DEUTERONOMY 15:7–8

"PASTOR, I NEED HELP." THE WOMAN ON THE PHONE INTRODUCED herself softly and tried not to cry. She was obviously embarrassed and having a hard time telling her story for what was probably the twentieth time. "My husband left me last month with two children, and I don't know where to find him. Our rent is past due and the landlord just gave me an eviction notice. I am so scared, and I don't know where to turn. Please help me."

My heart aches that my church can't do enough. Few churches can. The need is so large and our resources so small. God opens doors to provide more, but even that "more" is only a beginning. Meanwhile, I and many other pastors like me still have to tell some families that we can't help them and apologetically give them the numbers of a few places where they may have better luck.

Pastors spend a great deal of time fielding calls from people within the community who need various types of assistance. In a given week, we might get half a dozen calls requesting help for groceries, rent assistance, utility bills, medical care, and a host of other needs. And while our congregations may have some money set aside for such purposes, the limited funds can't match the needs. And so we are forced to make choices about who is more deserving and who seems to be telling the truth and just how to split a very small pie into too many pieces.

Making judgments about who is more deserving of help is difficult. As those who are in need come to you, let the love of Christ shine through you. Pray for those who have come to you for help. Pray for guidance and wisdom in making the decisions and for greater provision in meeting the needs in your community. ☙

Don't worry—I'm a professional

In the presence of God and of Christ Jesus . . .
I solemnly urge you: . . . always be sober,
endure suffering, do the work of an evangelist,
carry out your ministry fully.

—2 TIMOTHY 4:1,5

AT THE CLOSE OF BIBLE STUDY, WE TOOK TIME TO SHARE PRAYER concerns. We went around the room, ending with one of the college girls. She added the name of a friend of hers who was going through a hard time. I noticed that she herself was almost crying as she spoke, and that worried me. At the end of the prayer, I turned to her and gently probed, letting her know I was concerned for her.

Within a few moments, she was weeping, clearly overwhelmed by the magnitude of her friend's problems. He was threatening to hurt himself, and she was his only ally—a pretty big burden to carry. As I helped her get the assistance she needed to help him, you could almost see that a weight was lifted from her shoulders. Later, on the way home, a friend said to me, "I could never have done what you did. I was so uncomfortable that I couldn't have brought it to the conclusion that you did. I am glad you were there."

It is no small thing when pastors first begin to notice that our pastoral skills are improving. Almost two years passed before I finally saw that I gotten better at this ministry than I used to be. I was excited and encouraged that I had actually made progress! I had thought I was doomed to stay in the awkward, first-year-out-of-seminary, don't-have-a-clue mode.

Praise God when you begin to feel more confident about the work that you have been given to do. Be thankful for God's faithfulness, and pat yourself on the back for not giving up! ❧

61

Butterflies for breakfast

I am the vine, you are the branches.
Those who abide in me and I in them bear much fruit,
because apart from me you can do nothing.

—JOHN 15:5

ON SUNDAY MORNINGS, I DON'T EAT A REAL BREAKFAST. IN FACT, I consider myself fortunate if I can choke down anything at all. Usually the most I can handle is a cup of hot tea. Although I am somewhere between being an extrovert and an introvert, Sunday mornings make me nervous. I want everything to go according to plan—which, of course, rarely happens.

Invariably, I have a last-minute panic about my sermon, for which I can always imagine a dozen improvements in the last fifteen minutes before worship begins. If we are going to have a special speaker, my panic is different—but worse. I will wake up at least two or three times during the night, agonizing over whether I gave the correct directions, the right time for services, and so on. It makes for a miserable night for my husband and me.

In a recent, concerted effort to give the worship service over to God, I confessed the sin of my own pride and let go of the following Sunday's worship. The service fared much worse than even I could have anticipated. A dear elderly member of the congregation stood to give an announcement and spoke for *twelve minutes,* give or take a few seconds. Then we sang a new hymn, one which, up to that point, had been a favorite of mine. The organist, pianist and worship leader all decided to follow different paths, however. Finally, as I led the morning prayer, a cacophony of infant wailing filled the air for several minutes. I ended the service wondering if I hadn't been better off worrying.

But after the benediction, as I stood in the receiving line to greet my members, more than one spoke of how powerful the service had been to them and how much they had appreciated the message. Apparently, I was the only one who had missed the blessing.

As pastors, we are not the ones who are ultimately responsible for worship; God is. As long as we are well-prepared and the service is covered in prayer, we can rest easy. Trust God to meet you and your members in worship. Pray now for your biggest concern about the worship service, and release it into God's care.

62

Sweat of my brow

For we are God's servants, working together;
you are God's field, God's building.

—1 CORINTHIANS 3:9

WIPING SWEAT FROM MY BROW, I WONDERED ALOUD JUST HOW MANY cans of green beans one food pantry needed. After emptying yet another box of canned vegetables, I groaned as I discovered a fourth box of chicken noodle soup. Jennifer, a church member who had offered to help restock the pantry shelves on her day off, laughed when she uncovered another fifty boxes of macaroni and cheese. As we worked, we talked about good books, about what it was like growing up in this area, and about what it was like to leave and then come home.

While organizing can after can of mixed vegetables, we enjoyed a sense of camaraderie and partnership. By the time we were finished unpacking boxes, our backs ached from bending over time and time again, and we were tired. It had been a busy few hours. Still, I felt good to have accomplished so much, and the task had provided a good opportunity to get to know Jennifer a little better. I could have done the project by myself or with my spouse's help, but I would have missed out on the chance to work alongside one of my members. Those hours weren't earth-shattering stuff, but the morning did add another link in forging a relationship with Jennifer.

The more time members spend with their pastor, the greater their trust levels are. They are more likely to bring up the burdens of their heart with the pastor with whom they are working side by side on a project than they are to make a counseling appointment with a leader who is a relative stranger. With every project that needs to be done, we should look for opportunities to invite our members to participate.

Consider how God might want to use you to build new relationships with some folks you have not gotten to know very well. Pray that the Lord would lead you to take advantage of everyday tasks and ordinary moments to cultivate friendships with your members. ❧

63

A world of hurt

God is our refuge and strength,
a very present help in trouble.
Therefore we will not fear,
though the earth should change,
though the mountains shake in the heart of the sea;
though its waters roar and foam,
though the mountains tremble with its tumult.

—Psalm 46:1–3

I sat dumbfounded in front of the television set as I watched scenes from another high school shooting. Another senseless rampage on innocent children and faculty. Tears came to my eyes as I stopped to pray for families, for rescue workers, for the lives that would be changed as the death toll rose. I tried to imagine their terror but couldn't even begin to conceive what the students, parents, and community must be feeling. Within a few hours, the telephone began ringing with members wanting to know if I had heard the news.

In the days that followed, the shooting was the topic of conversation at Bible studies, Sunday school classes, and informal talks over coffee. How safe were our kids? Could something like that happen here, in our town? How do we protect our children? What kind of world do we live in where kids hunt each other down? The conversations couldn't have been avoided even if I had tried.

As pastors, we may be amazed to realize that our people need to be comforted in the wake of a tragedy that has occurred a thousand miles away. And yet, they do. They feel frightened and vulnerable—afraid for their children and grandchildren, suddenly very much aware that the world feels a little more threatening than it did the day before. They need the opportunity to express their concerns and vent their outrage. Where better than in the church, and whom better than to their pastor?

How do you respond when local and national tragedies occur? Do you offer enough opportunities for your members to process the events? Be available to listen when you are needed. Seek the comfort of Christ for your people.

64

Life on the edge

He gives power to the faint,
and strengthens the powerless.
Even youths will faint and be weary,
and the young will fall exhausted;
but those who wait for the LORD shall renew their strength,
they shall mount up with wings like eagles,
they shall run and not be weary,
they shall walk and not faint.

—ISAIAH 40:29–31

AS I CRADLED THE TINY INFANT NOT BIGGER THAN MY HAND, I gingerly wrapped her body in a receiving blanket and closed the drawer where she had been laying in the morgue. Laying her in the bassinet, I quietly wheeled her down to the hospital chapel for her funeral. I stepped on my toe with the heel of my shoe, willing myself not to display any emotion. If I started crying, I wasn't sure I would be able to stop.

The infant's mother, a teenager addicted to crack cocaine, came in on the arm of her boyfriend and dealer, who may or may not have been the infant's father. The mother looked as though she had just gotten high on her way down from her hospital room. She had been twenty-eight weeks pregnant and her water had broken, but it had taken her two days to get to the hospital.

A friend of mine slipped in the door of the chapel and gave me an encouraging nod. I cleared my throat and willed myself to begin. At that moment, I wasn't sure I could. This was too difficult. What I wanted to do instead was run down the hallway and out the door to a job where I didn't have to bury babies. Where I wasn't furious at seventeen-year-old crack addicts. Where the work just wasn't so hard. Yet, I knew that even babies born too soon deserve to be acknowledged. I just wasn't sure I was the one able to do it.

But in the end, I did, just as I have done every hard thing since. God has been faithful. But being in the ministry often means confronting the raw edges of life and death and horror from which most people are insulated. And if we as pastors are not willing to be there for God's people, then who will? Pray that you would make yourself available for whatever the Lord calls you to do, and that God will be faithful to give you the grace and strength needed to do the work, no matter how difficult the task. ❧

65

Hebrew verbs and committee meetings

For God is my witness,
how I long for all of you with the
compassion of Christ Jesus.

—PHILIPPIANS 1:8

MY STUDY CARREL WAS HIDDEN BEHIND ANCIENT TREATISES ON eschatology in the west wing of the third floor. I could sit for hours there in the musty, time-worn, seminary library. Back then, I had all the time I needed to pursue whatever assignments were given. Seminary was challenging, and although I was glad to be done, now I find myself occasionally yearning for those days.

Once in a while, I find that I miss the friendly banter and discussions on even the most esoteric aspects of philosophy, the feeling of the sun warm on our backs as we were awed by unveiling the mysteries of reading the Bible in its original languages. Evaluating success and failure was easy; the grade book told us clearly. And if our grades dipped, forgiveness was just another test away.

Pastoring is a far different world. Errors are not so easily forgiven. A slip of the tongue can take months to repair. Success can be difficult to measure. The job feels lonely sometimes. Homesickness can be overwhelming.

And yet, God is faithful. I don't really want to be back in seminary. If I were, I would miss preaching. I'd miss officiating at weddings and watching people I love grow in their faith. I'd miss watching Christmas pageants and basketball league tournaments and teaching Sunday school classes. But most of all, I'd miss being where Jesus has called me to be.

What do you miss about seminary? What has been difficult to replace? What brings you joy in the ministry? Thank God for those blessings. ❧

A round peg

Nevertheless I am continually with you;
you hold my right hand.

—Psalm 73:23

The laughter filled the room as stories flowed from years gone by. These are good friendships that have lasted through decades of change and growth, loss and joy. "Remember when . . ." starts one woman, and the rest listen expectantly, curious about what anecdote she will recall. The story is even better than they remembered, and they roar with laughter, some wiping away tears. My husband winks and smiles at me from across the room. At the annual Sunday school Christmas party, pastor and spouse are expected to attend.

But we don't know these stories. They don't mean much to us. They happened long ago, often to people we have never met. Sometimes the stories exclude us because, after all, pastors (and their families) come and go. I fake a polite smile and feel, for the moment, a little homesick. I long for the familiarity of my own friends and family and of our shared history. That is perhaps what I miss the most in my calling to be a pastor.

However much a place feels like home, sometimes as new pastors we are confronted with the reality that it really isn't. Sometimes we spend the holidays alone because we're too far away from our extended families and friends and no one else thought to ask us to dinner. We may feel as though we are walking between two worlds—an important part of people's lives on one hand, especially in times of excitement or grief, but forever an outsider on the other.

When you experience those feelings of homesickness and isolation, remember that your true home is with God, and in God only will you find total acceptance and comfort. Draw near to the Lord. ❧

Jack-of-few-trades

Do all things without murmuring and arguing,
so that you may be blameless and innocent,
children of God without blemish in the midst
of a crooked and perverse generation,
in which you shine like stars in the world.

—Philippians 2:14–15

Boring, or carpenter, bees are particularly destructive to wooden buildings. I never knew that before; now I do. We have fifteen holes in the church overhang to prove it. Also, each fire extinguisher ought to be inspected every six months, but the church's had not been tested for eight years. We didn't even know where they were located. Our insurance agent would not have been pleased. And you wouldn't believe the complexities of tax law regarding paying social security for employees of the church. I didn't. Now I even know which form to file.

When I came to my first church, armed with my shiny new master of divinity degree and a few years' experience as a youth pastor, I was ready for anything—or so I thought. My sermons were planned for the first six months, and I had my pocket-sized Bible to carry on pastoral calls. Yet, all the things I spent four years of seminary learning take up only about a quarter of my time. The rest, I figure out as I go along.

In fact, every week I seem to learn a new aspect of my work. In larger churches, I suppose that pastors can have their areas of expertise and other staff members do the "dirty work." In most churches, however, even a secretary is an unknown luxury. Thus, most of us pastors cannot afford to be specialists who only focus on the lofty tasks of sermon preparation and counseling. We dare not allow the mundane details of church life to be ignored.

Ask God for a willing heart to learn what you need to know in your new pastorate. Pray for a teachable spirit that is ready to absorb the seemingly insignificant aspects of your ministry. Ask God to help you avoid a negative attitude about how your valuable time should be spent.

68

You like me, you really like me!

So our aim is to please him always,
whether we are here in this body or
away from this body. For we must all stand
before Christ to be judged. We will each receive
whatever we deserve for the good or evil
we have done in our bodies.

—2 Corinthians 5:9–10, NLT

"Going through the counseling was like dating all over again. It really helped to get us talking again. Thank you," smiled the young wife. "We appreciated the time you spent with us. We just wanted you to know that." I leave the office for the evening, enjoying both the compliment and the cool breeze. I like to feel appreciated and valued; we all do.

We so want people to approve of our ministries and what we are doing, that sometimes we may catch ourselves bragging, just a little. "The numbers are up by 17 percent!" we'll say. "You know that we have six new families this year." And while we do need to present information about the status of the church, it can be dangerous for us to use church progress as an opportunity to toot our own horns.

While being aware of how people are responding to us and our leadership is important, the bottom line is that only one opinion really matters. Only one viewpoint can be the ultimate judge of our ministries, and that is Jesus'. Living and dying by opinion polls, even within our own churches, is a tough way to live. We may find that we preach on fluff topics just to make sure we don't offend anyone. Popularity contests too often compromise our leadership by forcing us to play safe. We want to be liked, but making our people happy isn't the goal of our ministry. Pleasing God is.

Accept compliments graciously, but realize that God's acceptance and approval of you matter the most. Corrie Ten Boom used to say that she gathered all of her compliments like flowers in a bouquet and gave them to the Lord every night. You, too, should seek the affirmation of the Lord in your ministry. Focus on God's will for you and for your people. ❧

69

Backtracking

Therefore, since we are justified by faith, we have peace with God through our Lord Jesus Christ, through whom we have obtained access to this grace in which we stand; and we boast in our hope of sharing the glory of God. And not only that, but we also boast in our sufferings, knowing that suffering produces endurance; and endurance produces character; and character produces hope, and hope does not disappoint us, because God's love has been poured into our hearts through the Holy Spirit that has been given to us.

—ROMANS 5:1–5

MY IDEAS WERE SO GOOD, THE PLAN SO FOOLPROOF, THAT I FELT SURE it would succeed. People were praising my intuitive thinking and original solutions. Then why was I immobilized? I was making little effort to put the project into motion.

"Dear God, bless this project," was how I had begun my prayer, but now, with head bowed, I confessed in the quietness of the darkened sanctuary. Instead of meeting God on bended knee *before* I had made my plans, I only sought the Lord's blessing afterwards. I so wanted to succeed that I had been bent on doing it on my own. I had wanted no help from anyone else in the church, much less from God. I wanted to succeed, to show everyone how smart, how talented I was.

And now I was afraid. Afraid even to try. Afraid to fail. Afraid that my ideas weren't big enough, weren't creative enough. That I wasn't . . . enough. I hated to admit that, deep down, I really doubted my abilities as a pastor. I played the role convincingly enough behind the scenes, but when the curtain opened, I doubted my ability to fulfill the part. I wondered how quickly my inadequacies would be discovered, exposing me as the fraud I suspected I was. Silent tears fell, clouding my glasses as I leaned forward, resting my elbows against the pew with folded hands under my chin. My pride had been keeping me from communion with God.

As pastors, we are far worse off when we are convinced of our abilities than when we admit our weaknesses as sinners in need of a gracious God. What inadequacy or sin do you need to confess? Is anything, right now, hindering you from a closer walk with the Lord? ❧

70

But she's so...

We try to live in such a way that no one will be
hindered from finding the Lord by the way we act,
and so no one can find fault with our ministry.
In everything we do we try to show
that we are true ministers of God.
We patiently endure troubles and hardships
and calamities of every kind.

—2 CORINTHIANS 6:3–4, NLT

"THAT'S NICE, CINDY," I SAID, FRUSTRATION EVIDENT IN MY TONE. "Real Christian attitude you've got there."

The room grew silent as Cindy turned and shot me a look that registered disbelief and irritation. We were sitting in a committee meeting, and I had just about had it. Every time a new idea was suggested, Cindy bad-mouthed it. Some were great ideas and some were not so great, but she ridiculed every one. One new member had tried to volunteer two suggestions, only to be told quickly, "We tried that already and it didn't work."

Nevertheless, no matter how much she irritated me, my comment wasn't exactly appropriate. I knew it as soon as the words were out of my mouth. Obtaining forgiveness for that mistake took some time. When I am in committee meetings now and I am fighting the urge to use a sharp tongue, I stop and quietly pray, "Lord, help me to show your love. Let your love pour through me."

As pastors, we should never give voice to such scathing or judgmental thoughts, no matter how justified we feel the thoughts are. In tense situations, we might try to introduce some humor, to offer up a quick prayer for guidance, or just bite our tongues. I didn't do any of those things, and I regretted it.

During what situations is someone more likely to find fault with you and your ministry? In other words, where are you most likely to fall short and to act or speak impatiently? How can covering those times with prayer make a difference? ❧

71

Sowin' seeds

What then is Apollos? What is Paul? Servants through whom you came to believe, as the Lord assigned to each. I planted, Apollos watered, but God gave the growth. So neither the one who plants nor the one who waters is anything, but only God who gives the growth.

—1 CORINTHIANS 3:5–7

I WASN'T SURE WHO WAS BEING PUNISHED MORE, JOHN OR I. ON THAT crisp autumn day, my company for the afternoon was a stubborn, rebellious teenager, armed with a rake and a trash bag. He had been suspended from school for disrespect (again!), and his parents had worried that if he were left alone at home all day, he would find more trouble. And so, because I pictured myself as a rescuer of even the most hardened kid, I had agreed to "babysit" him for the week.

The days stretched into a much longer week than I had originally anticipated. John grudgingly agreed to rake leaves, although his efforts served more to flatten the leaves than to actually relocate them. His heart was hardened against things of the Spirit, and by the end of the week, he was no "better" than when he had arrived. His parents were appreciative of my watchful eye, but I was disappointed that his behavior and character exhibited no obvious changes.

If the truth were told, I would have to admit that the same was true for some other young people I had worked with for a year or more. I loved the kids. We talked, they trusted me, and yet, a couple of them I just could not reach. I felt that I had failed them. I had a hard time giving them over to the Lord and trusting that God's will would be done.

What seeds are you not willing to let take root? Pray that the Lord would keep you humble and away from an exaggerated sense of your own importance. Be willing to be the planter of seeds and not the reaper who receives the rewards. ❧

72

Take this thorn...

Dear brothers and sisters, honor those who are your leaders in the Lord's work. They work hard among you and warn you against all that is wrong. Think highly of them and give them your wholehearted love because of their work. And remember to live peaceably with each other.

—1 THESSALONIANS 5:12–13, NLT

MY FIRST CHURCH WOULD HAVE BEEN DOING FINE, IF NOT FOR THIS one man. He was a bitter old man, paralyzed from an illness and perpetually angry. He also happened to be the treasurer, which meant that every member of the staff had to deal with him on a regular basis. He paid whatever bills he deemed worthy of paying, regardless of what the church body had approved in the budget.

What was even more frustrating was that he would drive to the church every weekday morning and park outside the office, under a nearby tree. He would pull out an old notebook and a pencil and keep notes of when each staff member would arrive and depart—our own personal time clock. It was disconcerting to pass him in the parking lot. I always tried to get there before he did, but in four years of employment, I never was successful.

In many churches, one or two of the church leaders are determined to make the pastor's life difficult. Generally this is done out of a deep love for the church. Often, the individuals are longtime members who feel threatened by change. Being patient with these folks is tough. Occasionally, a real problem develops when a church leader is *not* acting in the best interest of the church. But as pastors, we may struggle to recognize that just because other leaders don't agree with us, that doesn't mean they are bad leaders.

Pray for your church leaders today. Pray for their walks with the Lord and for their leadership abilities, and give thanks for their ministry to the church. Ask God to keep you from being resentful of any of the leaders.

73

Toughing it out

Be glad for all God is planning for you.
Be patient in trouble, and always be prayerful.

—ROMANS 12:12, NLT

I WAS GETTING GOOD AT PLANNING FUNERALS. EVERY WEEK OR SO, I pulled out my trusty green notebook planner, poised my pen, and asked the same questions. I would look family members in the eye, offer my most sympathetic look, and softly ask to be invited in their lives. "Tell me about your loved one," I would say. "Talk about what they meant to you. What made him special? What gave her joy?" The questions were rote, although the families' answers differed.

As another day dawned, another funeral beckoned. Slipping my black jacket over my shoulders, I tried to shrug off my bleak mood. I couldn't do it. I was spiritually drained and emotionally exhausted. My job just demanded too much from me. I was no longer sure that I was up to the task. Even as I slipped my funeral manual into my pocket and headed for the door, what I *wanted* to do was crawl back into bed, pull the covers over my head, and dream of a job where I didn't have to deal with heartache, tragedy, and brokenness.

Sometimes, the key to survival in our pastoral ministries is just to set our jaws and go on faithfully, trusting, despite outward circumstances, that God is on hand to help. As pastors we trust that God, who raised Jesus from the dead, can also change our circumstances because that same God hears our voices.

Choosing joy through hope instead of despair, choosing patient endurance in times of affliction, and choosing faithfulness in prayer—all these are decisions of the will. Pray that God will give you the strength to make such choices and to press on toward the goal to which you are called in Christ Jesus. ❧

74

A new coat of paint

The Lord, *your God, is in your midst, . . .*
he will rejoice over you with gladness,
he will renew you in his love;
he will exult over you with loud singing. . . .

—Zephaniah 3:17

I was drawn to the bright, vivid colors as I loaded them into my shopping cart—purple, green, and pink bottles of paint. The paintbrushes and stencils were ready. I was going to paint my office, and a choir of angels would look over my shoulder as I worked. In recent weeks people had been coming into my office and commenting on the changes. A plant here, a new rug there. Finally, it was beginning to look less institutional and more like a welcoming place, more like . . . home.

For almost two years, I had left my office almost exactly the way I found it. Ecru walls, metal desk, rows of sagging wooden bookcases. Obligatory degrees were framed and hung on the wall, but that was the extent of my decorating. It was as though I didn't want to get too comfortable. I wasn't sure this place was really where I wanted to be. Surely, I thought, this was a stopping place on the way to somewhere different, somewhere . . . better.

And then it happened. I stopped wishing I was somewhere else. I felt something that seemed eerily close to contentment. I could agree to a three-year contract without hesitation. But most of all, I knew I was where God wanted me. I no longer had to know for how long and for what reason, nor did I need to map out a five-year plan. Instead, I just let God love me and delight in my obedience. When I succumbed to God's plan, my walk with the Lord grew more intimate.

As pastors, we can grow accustomed to being independent, even isolated. We hesitate to depend on anyone, even God, being sure that we know best. What we fail to recognize is that God is the one who has brought us thus far; God will be the one to move us on again. Until then, we are called to "bloom" where the Lord has planted us.

What area of your life needs God's attention? Does God have opportunities to delight in you and in your obedience? Are you "at home" where God has placed you?

75

Only so much we can do

Jesus said to the people, "I am the light of the world.
If you follow me, you won't be stumbling through the darkness,
because you will have the light that leads to life."

—John 8:12, NLT

"I know the church will want to support such a fine ministry as ours, Pastor," continued the well-clad gentleman in my office. "I know what a heart you and your flock have for the lost people in our community. If I could just have a few minutes of your time . . ." He wanted to come during the Sunday morning worship service and share about his mission projects and, of course, collect a love offering.

Shortly after he left, the phone rang. The caller, another pastor from the area, introduced himself and went on to explain his reason for calling. "I know you have only attended one of our organization's meetings in the last two years and we have never even met, but your name was brought up as a excellent candidate for the office of secretary."

A dozen more pleas came that same week in the mail. This Sunday school curriculum will revolutionize the Christian education department. This ministry resource will win the city to Christ virtually by itself. Don't miss this board meeting or that open house! Pastors can get discouraged having to turn so many people down. Some meetings *are* important to attend and some great ministries need to be promoted, but far more than we can accommodate beg for our time, energies, and resources.

Because of our limitations, pastors have to act as a filter and sift out so many seemingly worthwhile opportunities. Time is limited. So are the money and energy—not just yours as pastor but also that of your people. Know that how you spend your own resources, as well as the church's resources, is important to God. Ask the Spirit to help you keep God's vision for you and the church clear.

76

Stay out of the way

Now glory be to God! By his mighty power at work within us, he is able to accomplish infinitely more than we would ever dare to hope or ask. May he be given glory in the church and in Christ Jesus forever and ever through endless ages. Amen.

—EPHESIANS 3:20–21, NLT

A CHRISTIAN MUSIC VIDEO BLARED IN THE BACK CORNER OF THE room as streams of people began filtering through the doors. Soon, the back of the sanctuary was filled with rows and rows of people waiting for their turn in the food pantry. Fresh fruit, vegetables, bread, and more awaited those who needed them. One little girl was excited about getting a box of Jell-O, a luxury her family could not afford to buy. Still another child was looking forward to all the "neat" food his family could cook in the microwave of the hotel room where they lived.

In a given night, about seventy-five people received food from the pantry. It was hard to imagine that the ministry had only been open for a few weeks. Almost two hundred people were fed within the second month of its opening—and this was in a "good," middle-class neighborhood. What had started as a small spark of an idea soon grew into full-fledged reality. Seeing

God's hand at work in opening all the right doors was exciting. It was a *blessing* to see new people volunteering, needs being met, and most of all, lives being changed, one bag of groceries at a time.

As pastors, we need to pray for a united vision within our congregations for what God wants our churches to be doing in our communities. Where is the need in your neighborhood? Is it feeding the hungry? Housing the homeless? Mentoring the children? Are you tapping into the desire of God's heart? What changes might you need to make to more clearly hear God's voice? Pray for a discerning spirit and a willing heart—in you, yourself, and in your people. ❧

77

Falling away

"People are like grass that dies away;
their beauty fades as quickly as the beauty of wildflowers.
The grass withers,
and the flowers fall away.
But the word of the Lord will last forever."

—1 PETER 1:24–25, NLT

WHEN SAM WALKED IN THE ROOM THAT DAY, IT WAS HARD TO NOT TO drop your jaw in surprise. We had not seen him for several weeks, and obviously, the cancer was taking its toll. He was down to 114 pounds but looked to weigh far less. His clothes seemed many sizes too big, as if purchased for a man almost twice his size. They were, his wife whispered, the smallest size available in men's clothes. The bruising on his arms and face was a new development; his skin was so sensitive that towel-drying too briskly after a shower could bruise him for weeks.

I couldn't help wondering how long Sam would be with us. I could not imagine that he would be here when the autumn leaves began to turn. *Not that I wish him dead,* I quickly added in my thoughts. *I just hate to see him suffer.* Clearly, he was in a great deal of pain. Even the morphine was inadequate to dull the agony. And Sam was not alone in his struggle against the disease. On the following Monday morning, three of our members were receiving chemotherapy at the same hospital.

As the months roll by, pastors watch as our members begin to sicken and their health fails; their vitality drains away, replaced by the quiet stillness of preparations for death. As unpleasant as it is for us to watch our people suffer and die, the process is unavoidable. Some people are not healed. Disease and old age are mighty warriors. We may shy away from such situations because death and illness make us uncomfortable. One of the worst things we can do, however, is to abandon, physically or emotionally, our members, their family, and their friends when they need us. When we have the opportunity to walk with our people as they prepare to die, it is a difficult time, but it can also be powerful and meaningful.

Pray now for those in your congregation who are ill or elderly. In what ways can you assist them in their journey through illness and ultimately even to death? Pray that you might be fully present to those in need. ❧

78

Good-enough neighbor

[Jesus] said to him, "'You shall love the Lord your God with all your heart, and with all your soul, and with all your mind.' This is the greatest and first commandment. And a second is like it: 'You shall love your neighbor as yourself.' On these two commandments hang all the law and the prophets."

—Matthew 22:37–40

Being a Christian neighbor is much easier when you don't *have* neighbors. It is when you have people in close proximity that being neighborly becomes difficult. My family had had neighbors before and we had never experienced any problems, so we were not concerned when we moved into our new parsonage. We were aware that our neighbor's homestead held an assortment of old vehicles and even small buildings in varying stages of disrepair. We also knew that the man had a fondness for unusual animals, as was obvious by the llamas and peacocks who paraded in their pens. These seemed small things of little importance.

But we weren't ready for the guinea hens. Those creatures were new to us. Large, almost-flightless birds, they had an annoying preference for our property over their own. This would not have been a problem if they had been pleasant animals, but they weren't. They had a tendency to deposit copious amounts of waste right in front of the church doors as well as possessing the disturbing habit of screeching right under my bedroom window at 5:00 A.M. Often. As a pacifist, I surprised myself by wishing for a gun.

One morning on my way to make pastoral calls, I encountered the birds in the middle of the road, in the lane in which I was driving. I quickly calculated the amount of damage two good-sized birds would do to my van and decided the reward was worth the risk. I accelerated, then happened to glance to my left at my neighbor's fields, dismayed to find that he was outside, a plump, old man in worn-out overalls. He smiled and waved, oblivious to the carnage that was about to take place. His friendly wave did it. Clearly, he knew who I was. I swerved at the last possible second, sparing two animals that had most assuredly deserved to die.

As pastors, our witness to the people outside the church is as important, if not more so, than our witness to our members. In our communities, we are never *not* pastors. We are always "on." Other folks are looking at us to see what Christ looks like. What are you reflecting? Pray that you might reflect God's grace and love, not only in your church but in your community.

79

Bandaged fingers, wounded pride

And now, dear brothers and sisters, let me say one more thing as I close this letter. Fix your thoughts on what is true and honorable and right. Think about things that are pure and lovely and admirable. Think about things that are excellent and worthy of praise. Keep putting into practice everything you learned from me and heard from me and saw me doing, and the God of peace will be with you.

—PHILIPPIANS 4:8–9, NLT

TRYING UNSUCCESSFULLY TO HIDE MY BANDAGED HAND BY MY SIDE, I wanted to avoid raising unnecessary questions. The attempt was, of course, futile. "What did you do to your hand?" my flock asked me over and over again.

I was embarrassed and tried to dismiss their questions by saying, "No, it's really nothing, just a broken finger or two." No go. My "sheep" had become a school of piranhas, circling me, wanting to know exactly what had happened.

"Well," I tried to explain, "I was leaving church last night and as I opened the door, two of my fingers went back and I broke them."

My audience looked at me with disbelief. "That's what happened? I would make something up if I were you. A door? You couldn't walk through the door?" Snickers followed, and I knew that before long most people in our small church would know about my embarrassing injury.

On my way to church, I had considered lying about the incident. I considered making up a story in which I would appear less stupid. I even threw a few ideas around in my mind. But in the end, I just couldn't prevaricate. I had been preaching on integrity for the past several weeks, and my own words about truthfulness were still ringing in my ears.

And yet, I was embarrassed. I don't like to appear foolish, and there was no way to avoid it here. Pastors need an extra measure of grace to laugh with our folks. But, in the end, I chuckled too, and said, "You know, they need to put warning labels on those doors." And that sure was better than lying about it.

Allow your people to laugh with you. Do not be afraid to be real and fallible. Your people need to know that you are human, too. Save the goal of perfection for the Lord.

80

We need to talk

If another believer sins against you, go privately and point out the fault. If the other person listens and confesses it, you have won that person back.

—MATTHEW 18:15, NLT

PULLING OUT MY LEGAL PAD, I MADE A FEW NOTES ABOUT WHAT I wanted to say to Bob. *Not what I want to do,* I corrected myself. *What I need to do.* Over the last several weeks, I had received a few telephone calls from women in the church about Bob's behavior. It wasn't offensive or threatening, but a few woman and their husbands were uncomfortable. The time had come to confront him. I picked up the phone, slowly dialing his number.

When I spoke to Bob, I was clear and direct. Outlining the concerns that had been brought to my attention without mentioning names, I explained how his behavior had made some members feel. He was immediately embarrassed and chagrined, explaining that he was very sorry for the result of his behavior. Within a week he had apologized to the women, and the difficulties were eliminated. On the scale of church conflict, the situation had barely registered. Nevertheless, I had been reluctant to confront the issue.

Making the church a safe place for all people is one of the pastor's responsibilities. The church community needs to be free from hurtful behaviors, to the extent that we can make it so. And sometimes that means approaching a member about his or her behavior. Often, the confrontation is not easy, but it is necessary.

Can you think of a time when someone has been made uncomfortable by another's actions in your church? Pray for discernment about when to step in to maintain the environment of the church as a safe and healthy place. Claim God's courage when the time comes to address difficult situations.

81

Hungry sheep

I will give you shepherds
after my own heart,
who will feed you with
knowledge and understanding.
—JEREMIAH 3:15

MY OFFICE LOOKED LIKE A BOOKSTORE GONE BAD. CRUMBLED PAPERS littered the area surrounding the trash can. I diligently searched for notes scribbled on a dozen different sheets of paper, written at various times throughout the previous few months. Random books, my Bible, and an assortment of folders filled the carpet space around me. The time had come to plan my sermons for the next year, and the process was always a lengthy one.

But before I began in earnest, I pulled out my membership directory and looked through each page carefully. I considered each family and their struggles. In so many ways the year had been a tough one. Leukemia, tight finances, the death of a husband, an unsaved spouse, wayward children—each had taken its toll. And yet we had also welcomed new babies, new members of the flock, new plans for the future. The year had been a good one as well. Many of the concerns had already been etched in my heart, and yet I was reminded of them once again. Only then did I begin planning.

As pastors, we so want our messages and teaching to be what our people need. We may preach an entire series that is wonderful, but not relevant. The desire of our hearts is to feed our churches well, that the people might grow, both in spiritual maturity and in understanding. Pray that you might well discern the needs of your people. ❧

82

But I don't want to grow

Dear brothers and sisters, whenever trouble comes your way, let it be an opportunity for joy. For when your faith is tested, your endurance has a chance to grow. So let it grow, for when your endurance is fully developed, you will be strong in character and ready for anything.

—JAMES 1:2–4, NLT

I'VE NEVER BEEN A BELIEVER IN MURPHY'S LAW, YET IF SOMETHING can go wrong for me, almost inevitably it will. Minor irritation or major catastrophe, my life just seems to work out that way. Within a few months of my ministry, I had set a new record at our local office-supply company. Apparently no one before in the history of the company had any machine ever need service three times in eight days. Our church's photocopier was, the company said, a bad egg. Amazingly, so was the second one they sent. And while, usually, such mechanical problems are easy to deal with, some weeks even those challenges seem insurmountable.

As a general rule, I am content with my professional and spiritual progress. I rarely feel a need to test myself or to stretch in any real way. I am basically happy with the way I am and the way I think. And yet, I find that the Lord does not share the same opinion about my well-being! Instead, every time I turn around, to God seems to be providing another opportunity for me to grow. I must confess that I am not always appreciative of God's efforts on my behalf.

How has the Lord helped you to grow within the last few weeks or months? Have you welcomed such opportunities to grow in your faith? Say a prayers of thanks for a time God helped your endurance to grow. ❧

83

Left-over time

Take delight in the LORD,
and he will give you your heart's desires . . .
Be still in the presence of the LORD,
and wait patiently for him to act. . . .

—PSALM 37:4,7, NLT

EIGHT LITTLE GIRLS SHRIEKED AS THEY TOSSED THE WATER BALLOONS back and forth, breathlessly waiting as the brightly colored orbs fell toward them. Some of the girls were successful and caught them, with eyes closed and arms held out. Still others caught them and clutched too hard, breaking the fragile ball and sending rivulets of cool water running down their arms. Giggling, they begged for more. Even the shyest among them soon joined in the squeals of laughter. Relay races and "Duck, Duck, Goose" and "Simon Says" soon followed.

It was a rare thing, that perfect hour. To give children laughter. To sit on the ground and hug those girls and listen as they shared what had happened during the week. To teach about sharing and taking turns and empathy and friendship. The hour was, perhaps, a small thing, but it mattered to my daughter. It mattered to those wonderful, creative, strong, little girls.

As I left that night, picking up the remnants of balloons gone bad, I realized an important thing. I don't ever want to be in a place where I can't find space enough to do things like that—to spend an evening playing. As pastors, we should thank God if we can carve out enough space to enjoy life, gaze up at a setting sun, and listen to little girls ramble on about birthday parties and spiders and big brothers who act too silly.

Do you have those times? Create opportunities to share what you have to offer. Thank God for such moments of pure joy, of honest delight. ❧

84

Betrayed

My dear brothers and sisters, be quick to listen,
slow to speak, and slow to get angry. Your anger
can never make things right in God's sight.
So get rid of the filth and evil in your lives,
and humbly accept the message God has
planted in your hearts, for it is strong enough
to save your souls.

—JAMES 1:19–21, NLT

WORDS THAT NORMALLY I WOULD NEVER EVEN CONSIDER USING RAN through my mind. I wasn't sure I had ever heard anyone talk the way I wanted to. I was so angry that my teeth were clenched, my stomach was in knots, and my head throbbed. White-hot anger coursed through my veins and out of my pores. I couldn't recall ever having been that furious. Completely overwrought, I couldn't even go home. I knew I needed to cool off before my family had to bear the brunt of my emotions. Hours later, I caught myself planning my retort during my daughter's fifth birthday party.

Had it just been another church member who had treated me wrongly, I would not have been so infuriated. But this was different. This was a brother in the ministry. Clergy are supposed to stick together: advocates, friends, colleagues. And yet, he and I had had an uneasy relationship, and this was the last straw. Through a variety of means, he had actively worked to undermine my ministry. My repeated requests for him to change his behavior had not worked, and I had had it.

When a church member acts in a hurtful way, pastors can more easily write off the behavior as a sign of pain in that person's own life—and not necessarily as a reflection of our own ministry. But when the attack comes from a member of the clergy, somehow the injury is more painful and more difficult to understand. In my case, I didn't retaliate—but that doesn't mean I wasn't tempted! Playing by the rules can be tough when other folks won't do the same. And yet, because we only have to answer for ourselves and our own behavior when we stand alone before God, we want our name to be cleared of wrongdoing.

Has someone in the ministry been hurtful to you? Do you need to forgive them still? Are *you* being what *you* need to be to your brothers and sisters in the ministry?

85

Heart-talk

And this is my prayer, that your love may overflow
more and more with knowledge and full insight
to help you determine what is best, so that in the day of
Christ you may be pure and blameless, having produced
the harvest of righteousness that comes through
Jesus Christ for the glory and praise of God.

—PHILIPPIANS 1:9–11

"I USED TO THINK THAT I'D BE MARRIED BY AGE TWENTY, PREGNANT with child number one by twenty-two, and number two at twenty-four. That was back when I thought I had a say." With tears running down her cheeks, Shirley talked about her struggles with infertility and miscarriage. That night was the first time in my two-year ministry that she had let me into her heart and mind. Not incidentally, that night was also the first time I had suggested going out for a cup of coffee after a meeting.

Even in small churches, pastors have so little time with the majority of our people. Our days are overrun with paperwork, hospital visits, committee meetings, and telephone calls. Sitting down for a heart-to-heart with a parishioner is a too-rare event, with the exception of fleeting hours spent visiting with shut-ins, who seem to have all the time in the world. Working parents, and increasingly, even retirees with grandchildren or elderly relatives to care for, don't have much time for fellowship outside of Sunday morning worship.

In light of such realities in our own congregations, pastors ought to learn to be more creative in finding ways to get to know our people. And even more importantly, we ought not to waste our own time. Because we have such limited time to sit down one to one with our members, we can't waste that time in inconsequential discussions.

In my own ministry, I experience more of a sense of urgency in this matter of building relationships with my people. I still want to get to know my folks, but I want to know their hearts, not just their stock woes. I want to talk about the things of the spirit, about their journeys of faith. I do not want to read the obituaries of my members, knowing that I failed to encourage them in their faith when I had the opportunity. Time is short and I want to be faithful.

As pastors, we can't get so caught up in administrative tasks that we miss taking care of folks' spiritual needs. How can you improve your ability to reach people's hearts? Pray for opportunities to build stronger relationships with your church members. ❧

86

Losing a part

If one part suffers, all the parts suffer with it,
and if one part is honored, all the parts are glad.
Now all of you together are Christ's body, and each one
of you is a separate and necessary part of it.

—1 CORINTHIANS 12:26–27, NLT

HE HAD FOUGHT THE GOOD FIGHT. FOUR YEARS OF CANCER WAS A lot for anyone to take. An ideal patient, he had done everything the doctors told him to do. Every suggestion, even the most unusual ones, were grabbed by Todd and his wife in their hopes of beating the cruel disease. Together, they suffered through tests and treatments and hospitalizations because they wanted more—more time together. They hoped to enjoy Todd's retirement. After all, they had earned the chance to spend a decade or so traveling and relaxing and enjoying their family. But in the end, Todd's good days seemed to be fewer and fewer, sharply curtailing his ability to get out and about. His weight plummeted, dark bruises appeared on his skin, and we realized that he would not long be with us. In a relatively short time, late one summer night, cancer claimed him.

And after Todd's twenty-five years of active involvement in the church, his death claimed a part of the congregation as well. A deep sadness accompanies the loss of one of our own.

Church members cannot help but be reminded of special events and holidays in which the deceased had taken an active role. How much he loved to mow the lawn. How much she enjoyed helping in the nursery. Baby showers, anniversary services, fellowship dinners—they are woven into the fabric of our members' memories.

Spend time reminiscing with your members when they lose friends. Acknowledge their losses and be reminded of how painful it can be to see empty pews where good friends once sat. Pray for the friends of a church member who is sick right now. How can you minister to those friends as well as to the individual and his or her family? Take the community to the Lord in prayer.

Oh, baby

Be sure to do what you should, for then you will enjoy the personal satisfaction of having done your work well, and you won't need to compare yourself to anyone else. For we are each responsible for our own conduct.

—GALATIANS 6:4–5, NLT

"MEET ALLISON TUCKER," I SAID, SETTLING HER MORE COMFORTABLY in my arms. "I want you to get a good look at her. Have you ever seen so much hair on someone this little?" I walked up and down the main aisle, trying to hold the infant so that church members who craned their heads to get a better view could look at her face. She lay quietly, evidently unaware that she had passed into a stranger's arms. Appreciating the movement of our walk, she cooed loudly, kicking her legs in the air. The congregation was spellbound by her antics as I continued my musings.

"When we dedicate this child, I want you to have her image in your mind. I want you to think of Allison and her parents and consider whether you, personally, are committed to helping this child grow in her relationship with the Lord. This is not a nameless, anonymous kid; this is God's child and I want to know if you are willing to commit to her."

As I then dedicated the baby girl to the Lord, palpable emotion filled the room. There weren't many dry eyes in the place, least of all my own. The Holy Spirit was present and ministering during that service and God's presence was tangible in our hearts.

Allison's parents later commented that while they appreciated what I had said and how I had presented their daughter, what had most touched them was my own emotion. The fact that I had been moved by doing what I had done dozens of times already was meaningful for them.

As pastors, we may be tempted never to let our emotions get in the way while doing ministry. But when faced with the evidence that their pastor feels for them and with them, people will respond. Ask the Lord to help you be authentically *you* in worship. ❧

But they started it!

And you have forgotten the exhortation that addresses you as children—

"My child, do not regard lightly the discipline of the Lord,
or lose heart when you are punished by him;
for the Lord disciplines those whom he loves,
and chastises every child whom he accepts."

—HEBREWS 12:5–6

"MY CHILD, MY CHILD . . ." I COULD SENSE GOD'S WORDS AS CLEARLY as I felt the sun's warmth shining on my face. "Why do you let someone get you so angry? Why does anyone have that much control and power in your life? Give that power to me. I am the only one who needs to have control in your life." The Spirit's words touched my soul and pricked my conscience. I knew that what God was saying was right, of course. The message was just difficult to hear.

Perhaps I was hoping that the Lord's righteous indignation would condemn the one who had betrayed me. Perhaps I wanted the Lord's approval for the bitter feelings I had been nursing for days. And yet I knew better. I knew what God wanted *for* me and *from* me, and this resentment wasn't it. I knew I had only one thing to do: confess my sin to God and accept the Lord's chastening, however much I was reluctant to do so.

My attitude was reminiscent of my five-year-old's when I reprimand her. Sullen looks, stomped feet, and an angry march to her room often accompanied any rebuke my husband and I doled out. How I hate to admit that my attitude before the Lord isn't much better sometimes.

While my daughter doesn't always understand the love behind our admonishments, I should know better in my relationship with God. Accepting the Lord's correction with grace and a willing heart is necessary, but difficult. How willing are you to hear God's voice when you have been disobedient? What sin are you refusing to give over to God? Go to the Lord now, seeking to be in right relationship with God. ❧

89

Good behavior

Do not let anyone think less of you
because you are young.
Be an example to all believers
in what you teach, in the way you live,
in your love, your faith, and your purity.

—1 TIMOTHY 4:12, NLT

"AND THEN, AFTER SINGING SOME CHRISTIAN SONGS, THEY THREW IN some secular ones, including 'Honky-Tonk Woman.' After the last song, elderly Winslow slowly stood up and asked, 'What I want to know is—what, exactly, is a honky-tonk woman?'"

We laughed as a longtime church member related the story from years ago as we whiled away our shift in the church's food pantry. When a client came in, we smiled politely, directed her to the sign-in sheet, and then resumed our conversation.

As much as we have professed a desire to feed our clients not only physically, but spiritually as well, we didn't do a very good job that day. Rather than seizing the opportunity to initiate conversation with the strangers who came in, we found it easier to slip in a Christian video and let it do the "ministry" for us. With that obligation out of the way, we who staffed the pantry could continue to enjoy one another's company. I was just as likely as my members were to succumb to the temptation to hang back and catch up on the latest news with "our own."

Taking a hard look at what the church wanted to accomplish through this ministry and how my behavior was contributing (or *not* contributing) to that goal wasn't easy. How easily we forget that, as pastors, we are always being watched. Other people often model their behaviors after our own. Recognizing and accepting that reality is an awesome responsibility.

Ask God to help you examine any behaviors you display that do not glorify God. Seek to model Christ-like attitudes and attributes in your life for the sake of those who follow your example. ❧

90

Faithful words

Pay close attention to yourself and to your teaching;
continue in these things, for in doing this
you will save both yourself and your hearers.

—1 TIMOTHY 4:16

"GOD SPOKE TO ME SO CLEARLY THIS MORNING WHILE YOU WERE preaching, Angie," said a church member who had waited for me after the morning worship service. "God wanted me to tell you that he is pleased with your faithfulness in your preaching and wants you to continue to listen to what he has for you to say." Had the encouragement come from anyone else, I might have been skeptical. But this member was a man of God who walked closely with the Lord.

With tears in my eyes, I thanked my member. I had not told anyone else the struggles I was having to remain faithful to what I felt God was leading me to say. The last few weeks I had begun addressing topics that hit home for our families, issues such as obedience and forsaking false idols. The risk wasn't an easy one to make. Going out on the limb of faith wasn't as comfortable as hugging the sturdy trunk of familiar doctrine and affirmation.

When I first started preaching, week after week my sermons tended to focus primarily on God's grace and love. I only wanted to preach that which made my congregation feel good about themselves. While the themes were biblically true, the positive emphasis was an unbalanced diet and I knew it. Without also taking a hard look at what God requires of us, weeks of sermons on God's unfailing love made for spiritual milk. The people needed the meat of discipleship as well. On the other hand, preaching all justice, judgment, and righteous living without the seasoning salt of God's grace is not just difficult to swallow; it is downright indigestible. Serving up a balanced diet of the two is a real challenge.

As pastors, preaching faithfully the message God has entrusted to us can be rewarding, fulfilling, and terrifying. Spend time in God's presence. Craft each word with the Holy Spirit's assistance. Above all, be faithful to what *God* is calling you to preach.

91

Simple offerings

With Jesus' help, let us continually offer our sacrifice of praise to God by proclaiming the glory of his name.

—HEBREWS 13:15, NLT

WHEN I COME FOR A PASTORAL VISIT, SHE ALWAYS SERVES FRIED baloney sandwiches. I can count on it. I even look forward to it. The first time she served them, I was swamped by a flood of memories of my grandma's kitchen. I had not had those sandwiches in years. I had forgotten how good they were. Mary always goes to extra trouble, cutting the baloney just right and offering all kinds of side dishes, from Jell-O salad to cottage cheese. And she always gives me a cold glass of pop to wash it all down.

I have, of course, eaten fancier meals in more well-to-do homes, but rarely have I been treated with more kindness or truer hospitality. I know I am welcome in Mary's home. She and her family are pleased to have me sit at their table. And I am honored to be an invited guest. When I come, they do not just invite me into their home; they invite me into their hearts.

People will give their pastor what they have. For some folks, what they have is a lot of love and fried baloney sandwiches. For others, it will be sour grapes and a lifetime of bitterness. Grief, hurt, loneliness, joy, and compassion all come spilling out into a pastor's lap. Our job is to help pick up the pieces and offer the fragments to the Lord, knowing that God is more than able to receive whatever gifts we offer.

A pastor's unique privilege and responsibility is to be allowed an entry into the lives and kitchen tables of God's people. When your people open up to you and share, help them turn their hearts toward God and the state of their own spirits. Help them bring their offerings to the Lord. ☙

92

Always something

I exhort the elders among you to tend the flock of God that is in your charge, exercising the oversight, not under compulsion but willingly, as God would have you do it—not for sordid gain but eagerly.

—1 PETER 5:1,2

"THAT'S ALL YOU DO IS LEAVE. YOU RUSH IN HERE, SIT FOR A FEW minutes, and leave. As soon as you come in, you're gettin' ready to go," complained Edith. "You only come once a month." *Not true, I come every other Friday, without fail.* "And you stay five minutes if I'm lucky," she continued. *I always stay at least forty-five minutes. Always.*

Edith is home-bound and allowed to get out of the house only once a week or so. Company has become the highlight of her day. I was not surprised that she wanted me to visit more frequently, but I just couldn't do it.

After a morning in the office and a few pastoral calls in the afternoon, followed by sermon preparation and evening meetings, like most pastors, I was bushed. I had pushed myself to the limits of what I could do. Often, pastors have trouble deciding where to make the next call. So many needs demand our resources that we simply cannot do all that is expected of us.

And so, facing my own limitations and my member's needs, in the end, I let Edith choose: I would continue to come every other week for forty-five minutes, or I would come once a month and stay an hour and a half. The choice was hers. She felt better knowing that she had some input in the decision. She prefers a visit twice a month and looks for me every other Friday morning. I read her the paper, and we discuss her health and her concerns. I kneel in front of her, hold her hand, and pray with her as silent tears come down her cheeks. That is all that I can do. And it is enough.

Making decisions about how much time you can spend on visitation and who to see in that limited time is best made with the Lord's assistance. Review your last week of ministry. Were you able to make good use of your time? Pray that what you can do, although it seems little, will be enough. ❧

93

Hand in hand

And the peace of God, which surpasses all understanding, will guard your hearts and your minds in Christ Jesus.

—PHILIPPIANS 4:7

LEAVING THE DOWNTOWN LIBRARY, I TURNED TOWARD HOME. THE day had been full, and I had a lot to do before my daughter's birthday the next day. In the midst of my thoughts, I remembered Simon, who had been taken to the emergency room and admitted to the local hospital that morning.

In the final stages of leukemia, Simon wasn't feeling well. I had seen him just the night before at his home, so when I heard about his hospitalization, I assumed that his pneumonia had gotten worse. I usually wait until the following day to visit a newly admitted patient, but on this day, I felt compelled to go right away.

"God, is this what you want me to do?" And as clearly as if the words had been spoken, I knew that the answer was *yes*. A few minutes later, I pulled into the hospital parking lot, confident that God wanted me to be there. I spent an hour or so at the hospital that night, visiting and praying with Simon and his wife, bringing them a message of hope and love.

As pastors, we should never be so far away from God that we can't hear the Spirit's voice. Our job is not an easy one, even in the best of times. But if we allow ourselves to separate from the heart of God, the job becomes almost impossible.

What are *you* doing to maintain a close, intimate walk with the Lord? Are you able to recognize God's voice when the Spirit speaks to you? ❧

94

Solid rock

And I tell you, you are Peter, and on this rock I will build my church, and the gates of Hades will not prevail against it.

—MATTHEW 16:18

WHEN I AM AWAY FROM MY CHURCH FOR A FEW DAYS, I REALIZE THAT I am not as essential as I like to think I am. As amazing as it may seem, the church can function without me. While the congregation appreciates me and awaits my return, other people in the church are able to visit the sick, lead a committee meeting, or even preach in my absence. I am a good pastor, but I am not ultimately responsible for this church.

As pastors, we are humbled to understand that we are just one in a long line of shepherds. In a few years, whether five or fifteen or fifty, we will be just another name in a church's history book. In just a generation, members will not even remember our names. That reality doesn't make us irrelevant, but it does compel us to consider what kind of legacy we want to leave behind.

Do we want to leave our current pastorate knowing that people were brought into the Kingdom or that we succeeded in dividing the membership over the color of the new kitchen cupboards? When God calls me to leave this ministry, I want to know that I was faithful to the call to bring as many people as possible closer to God. With that as my goal, I am reminded that I do not want to be diverted from my task by power struggles, panic buttons, or painful battles.

When we as pastors understand that God is ultimately responsible for our churches, we are free to refocus our energies and resources and fall in line with what the Lord wants. Consider the legacy you are preparing. Are you spending your time and strength on issues that have no eternal significance? Pray that you would let go of such temporal matters and focus on God's plan for your church. ❧

95

Pray for whom?

Follow God's example in everything you do,
because you are his dear children. Live a life filled with
love for others, following the example of Christ, who loved you
and gave himself as a sacrifice to take away your sins.

—Ephesians 5:1–2, NLT

As I sat in the small auditorium and tried to listen to what the speaker was saying, my attention was drawn, time and time again, to someone with whom I was having difficulties. I missed most of the lecture as (again) I listed the reasons this person made me so angry. I knew that the people in my church knew how badly this man had acted and that they had been watching me closely to see how I would respond to him. The pressure to take the high road was enormous, and so slowly, I was letting go of the anger and allowing God to take care of the situation.

As a result, I was surprised that being in the presence of the man himself was enough to bring me to the boiling point again. *Oh Lord,* I prayed, *I just can't do this. You know what I'm thinking right now. You know how I'm feeling, and I so much want to be faithful to you, Lord. Help me!* And God's response to me was swift and sure: "Pray. Pray for him. Pray for his family. Pray for his walk with me."

I obeyed. And I found that I could not be angry and pray for that man at the same time. I tried. It was simply impossible. As I prayed for his wife, his children, his job, and his relationship with God, I couldn't be angry. I couldn't go to the Lord on his behalf and feel hatred toward him at the same time. Surrendering the situation to God was a wonderful release.

Whatever our sin, God wants to step in and take the burden for us. We are all tempted to sin against our brothers and sisters and against God. As pastors, our sinfulness can often be seen or exposed to members of our church. The consequences of that can be far-reaching, for us and for our people. Search your own heart. What sin have you not yet released to God? Take time now to confess. ❧

96

Loose lips

Not many of you should become teachers,
my brothers and sisters, for you know that we who teach
will be judged with greater strictness. For all of us
make many mistakes. Anyone who makes no mistakes
in speaking is perfect, able to keep the whole body
in check with a bridle.

—JAMES 3:1–2

IF I COULD HAVE TAKEN THE WORDS BACK, I WOULD HAVE. AS A relatively new youth pastor, I was out of my league when a mother came to me, suspecting that her teenage son was using drugs. Overwhelmed by the problem, I went to someone in the church for advice on how best to handle the situation in order to get the young man on the right road. Unfortunately, I erred—in giving that adviser the boy's name and in neglecting to emphasize that the information was confidential.

As might be expected, the consequences were disastrous. The information got back to the family that I was talking about their problems behind their backs. In the end, they would no longer speak to me and the son retreated even further. In retrospect, the choices I should have made were clear: obtaining permission before seeking someone else's assistance, avoiding use of the family's name, and going outside the church for help. One or all would have eased the situation and avoided the family's sense of betrayal.

As pastors, we need to be extremely careful with passing out information about our members. While material that comes out of counseling is obviously confidential, we may be needlessly careless with people's health information. We may want to share because we know others are concerned or even because we want to prove that we are "in the know." No matter how tempting the need to confide or gossip, pastors should refrain from passing on any information without asking permission from the persons involved.

Have you struggled to guard your lips carefully? Consider any specific concerns that you may have in this area, and ask God to give you wisdom and discretion. ❧

97

Not in vain

But thanks be to God, who gives us the victory through our Lord Jesus Christ. Therefore, my beloved, be steadfast, immovable, always excelling in the work of the Lord, because you know that in the Lord your labor is not in vain.

—1 CORINTHIANS 15:57–58

BEING IN MINISTRY HAS BEEN LIKE BEING ON A ROLLER COASTER. ONE moment I am resting in the Lord and sharing Christ with people and everything is wonderful. The next moment I am tongue-tied over what to say when someone is searching for faith or I am frustrated by a lack of enthusiasm for a pet project of mine. Each week is different. Some are weeks of rest and days full of opportunities to plan and pray and dream. Other weeks are strings of days when I leave for work early in the morning and don't come home until late at night, with concerns that even interrupt my dreams.

Focusing on the big picture is difficult for pastors! We agonize over every small detail in church life. Are the committee reports going to be ready before the business meeting since we switched the date? Is the new budget going to be approved, or will it get stalled in the finance committee? In the midst of such chaos,

God wants to tap us on the shoulder and remind us that our work is not in vain. God does not want us to be distracted from simple trust in the divine plan. We need to be reminded that the Holy Spirit is working, even when we cannot see evidence of God's presence. Our goal as pastors is that we would use each action of ministry as an offering to the Lord.

Rest in the promise that you are in God's hands and that God does everything well. ❧

98

Fellow servants

May the God of steadfastness and encouragement grant you to live in harmony with one another, in accordance with Christ Jesus, so that together you may with one voice glorify the God and Father of our Lord Jesus Christ. Welcome one another, therefore, just as Christ has welcomed you, for the glory of God.

—Romans 15:5–7

From the beginning, she made me uncomfortable. Her tone was adversarial, and her demeanor was haughty. Being with her was difficult. She smoked, spoke loudly, and was downright mean if she felt slighted in any way. I would come home from committee meetings with my stomach in knots when she was upset about something. Sheila was a difficult person to like.

I hate to admit my prejudices. Actually, I hate to admit I have so many of them. I am ashamed of just how critical I can be. I am critical of people who smoke, who let crying babies stay in the worship service, who are inflexible, and who are hypercritical! My inward reactions to people can be territorial and petty and downright ugly. I like folks who make me feel comfortable, and I dislike those who appear to threaten my interests.

But I am learning that I miss out when I write people off. If I fail to honor someone whom God is using, my disrespect is an insult to our Lord. And when I judge folks, I am no longer interested in what they have to offer. In cutting myself off from them, I may miss God speaking through them.

As pastors we need to choose to accept our people as they are and to appreciate how God is using them for the good of the body of Christ. Pray that the Lord would continue to teach you about your own prejudices and attitudes. Seek to enjoy the blessing of unity. Pray that you might learn to appreciate all the people whom God has given into your care. ☙

99

Growing pains

We always thank God for all of you and pray for you constantly.
As we talk to our God and Father about you,
we think of your faithful work, your loving deeds,
and your continued anticipation of our Lord Jesus Christ.

—1 THESSALONIANS 1:2–4, NLT

HOW CAN I APPLY THIS TEXT TO MY STRUGGLES? HOW DO I DISPLAY (or fail to display) these characteristics in my own life? What has been the most difficult area of my life to give over to God? Where are some of the places that I am likely to allow sin a foothold? These random notes and scribbles may not make it to the final text of my sermon, but they are a part of its underlying message. I preach where my heart is. I counsel from the Word of God etched in my own life. I cannot separate God's word to my people from God's word to me.

In the same way that my life affects my ministry, my ministry context affects my life. Never could I walk away from this place unchanged. I am a better person because I pastor here. The situations, circumstances, people, and conversations have stretched me, helped me, and changed me. As God continues to mold me more and more into the likeness Jesus Christ, God also provides opportunities for me to grow in my faith. But I also have to be willing to allow God to be at work in my heart, to encourage the Spirit to come in and root out that which separates me from God, to be willing to walk with my people with open arms and a loving spirit.

Sometimes any other position seems easier than the pastorate—times when a career in other fields seems tempting. More lucrative salaries, more prestige, and/or greater autonomy are all appealing. But the bottom line is that, as individuals, we need to be where God has called us to serve. And God has called you to *this* place, not only for the sake of the church, which needs what you uniquely bring, but also for your own sake—because you need the church. God knows that you need what these people will bring to your walk.

Has your church helped you develop in your walk with God? Be thankful for God's continuing faithfulness and providence through your people—through *God's* people.

100

Coming home

Jesus came and told his disciples, "I have been given complete authority in heaven and on earth. Therefore, go and make disciples of all the nations, baptizing them in the name of the Father and the Son and the Holy Spirit. Teach these new disciples to obey all the commandments I have given you. And be sure of this: I am with you always, even to the end of the age."

—MATTHEW 28:18–20, NLT

FROM THE FRONT PORCH OF THE LODGE, I COULD SEE THE GREAT Smoky Mountains—a breathtaking view on what was, quite possibly, a perfect morning. The sun was just beginning to stretch out its arms, and a handful of birds chirped nearby. For six more glorious days, we would be hidden away, tucked in a friend's getaway home, which is fit for royalty and loved by our family. We were on what could best be described as a well-earned vacation. The phone didn't ring during dinner and committee meetings were far away. There were no proposals, projects, budgets, or contracts to be had.

It was *good* to be away and to enjoy my family—to revel in the beauty of creation, the wonderment of my daughter, and in the good nature of my husband, to remember that we have been made for one another. Bonfires and bunk beds, S'mores and sleepy stories, hiking and hot tubs—it was all good time spent with this family of mine.

And yet, in the quiet of the morning, I wondered about my other family—the one I left behind. I wondered if Tanya's blood count would be high enough for a chemotherapy treatment that week. I wondered who Edith would call when she was lonely. I wondered how Ray was coping since his wife had had to enter the nursing home. I wondered, too, how Dwain and his young wife had celebrated their first anniversary last weekend. As my folks, one by one, came to mind, I bowed my head and prayed for them, giving them into the Lord's care. They too, as much as my spouse and child, have been given to me for safekeeping by the Lord, and how I do enjoy them. I don't want to forget that.

Our people are a gift given by our Lord and Savior. A pastor's prayer should be that we might be found faithful to the task to which God has called us. May you and I both love God's children in Jesus' name. ❧

SCRIPTURE INDEX

Referenced by devotion number